Drugs and Sports

POINT
COUNTERPOINT

Drugs and Sports

Alan Marzilli

SERIES CONSULTING EDITOR
Alan Marzilli, M.A., J.D.

CHELSEA HOUSE
PUBLISHERS
An imprint of Infobase Publishing

Drugs and Sports

Chelsea House
An imprint of Infobase Publishing
132 West 31st Street
New York NY 10001

Library of Congress Cataloging-in-Publication Data

Marzilli, Alan.
  Drugs and sports / by Alan Marzilli.
      p. cm. — (Point/counterpoint)
  Includes bibliographical references and index.
  ISBN 978-0-7910-9553-9 (hardcover)
  1. Doping in sports. 2. Athletes—Drug use. I. Title. II. Series.
  RC1230.M375 2008
  362.29—dc22   2008018757

Chelsea House books are available at special discounts when purchased in bulk
quantities for businesses, associations, institutions, or sales promotions. Please call
our Special Sales Department in New York at (212) 967-8800 or (800) 322-8755.

You can find Chelsea House on the World Wide Web at
http://www.chelseahouse.com

Series design by Keith Trego
Cover design by Keith Trego and Jooyoung An

Printed in the United States of America

Bang NMSG 10 9 8 7 6 5 4 3 2 1

This book is printed on acid-free paper.

All links and Web addresses were checked and verified to be correct at the time of
publication. Because of the dynamic nature of the Web, some addresses and links
may have changed since publication and may no longer be valid.

Alan Marzilli, M.A., J.D.
Birmingham, Alabama

The POINT/COUNTERPOINT series offers the reader a greater understanding of some of the most controversial issues in contemporary American society—issues such as capital punishment, immigration, gay rights, and gun control. We have looked for the most contemporary issues and have included topics—such as the controversies surrounding "blogging"—that we could not have imagined when the series began.

In each volume, the author has selected an issue of particular importance and set out some of the key arguments on both sides of the issue. Why study both sides of the debate? Maybe you have yet to make up your mind on an issue, and the arguments presented in the book will help you to form an opinion. More likely, however, you will already have an opinion on many of the issues covered by the series. There is always the chance that you will change your opinion after reading the arguments for the other side. But even if you are firmly committed to an issue—for example, school prayer or animal rights—reading both sides of the argument will help you to become a more effective advocate for your cause. By gaining an understanding of opposing arguments, you can develop answers to those arguments.

Perhaps more importantly, listening to the other side sometimes helps you see your opponent's arguments in a more human way. For example, Sister Helen Prejean, one of the nation's most visible opponents of capital punishment, has been deeply affected by her interactions with the families of murder victims. By seeing the families' grief and pain, she understands much better why people support the death penalty, and she is able to carry out her advocacy with a greater sensitivity to the needs and beliefs of death penalty supporters.

The books in the series include numerous features that help the reader to gain a greater understanding of the issues. Real-life examples illustrate the human side of the issues. Each chapter also includes excerpts from relevant laws, court cases, and other material, which provide a better foundation for understanding the arguments. The volumes contain citations to relevant sources of law and information, and an appendix guides the reader through the basics of legal research, both on the Internet and in the library. Today, through free Web sites, it is easy to access legal documents, and these books might give you ideas for your own research.

Studying the issues covered by the Point-Counterpoint series is more than an academic activity. The issues described in the book affect all of us as citizens. They are the issues that today's leaders debate and tomorrow's leaders will decide. While all of the issues covered in the Point-Counterpoint series are controversial today, and will remain so for the foreseeable future, it is entirely possible that the reader might one day play a central role in resolving the debate. Today it might seem that some debates—such as capital punishment and abortion—will never be resolved.

However, our nation's history is full of debates that seemed as though they never would be resolved, and many of the issues are now well settled—at least on the surface. In the nineteenth century, abolitionists met with widespread resistance to their efforts to end slavery. Ultimately, the controversy threatened the union, leading to the Civil War between the northern and southern states. Today, while a public debate over the merits of slavery would be unthinkable, racism persists in many aspects of society.

Similarly, today nobody questions women's right to vote. Yet at the beginning of the twentieth century, suffragists fought public battles for women's voting rights, and it was not until the passage of the Nineteenth Amendment in 1920 that the legal right of women to vote was established nationwide.

What makes an issue controversial? Often, controversies arise when most people agree that there is a problem, but people disagree about the best way to solve the problem. There is little argument that poverty is a major problem in the United States, especially in inner cities and rural areas. Yet, people disagree vehemently about the best way to address the problem. To some, the answer is social programs, such as welfare, food stamps, and public housing. However, many argue that such subsidies encourage dependence on government benefits while

FOREWORD

unfairly penalizing those who work and pay taxes, and that the real solution is to require people to support themselves.

American society is in a constant state of change, and sometimes modern practices clash with what many consider to be "traditional values," which are often rooted in conservative political views or religious beliefs. Many blame high crime rates, and problems such as poverty, illiteracy, and drug use on the breakdown of the traditional family structure of a married mother and father raising their children. Since the "sexual revolution" of the 1960s and 1970s, sparked in part by the widespread availability of the birth control pill, marriage rates have declined, and the number of children born outside of marriage has increased. The sexual revolution led to controversies over birth control, sex education, and other issues, most prominently abortion. Similarly, the gay rights movement has been challenged as a threat to traditional values. While many gay men and lesbians want to have the same right to marry and raise families as heterosexuals, many politicians and others have challenged gay marriage and adoption as a threat to American society.

Sometimes, new technology raises issues that we have never faced before, and society disagrees about the best solution. Are people free to swap music online, or does this violate the copyright laws that protect songwriters and musicians' ownership of the music that they create? Should scientists use "genetic engineering" to create new crops that are resistant to disease and pests and produce more food, or is it too risky to use a laboratory to create plants that nature never intended? Modern medicine has continued to increase the average lifespan—which is now 77 years, up from under 50 years at the beginning of the twentieth century—but many people are now choosing to die in comfort rather than living with painful ailments in their later years. For doctors, this presents an ethical dilemma: should they allow their patients to die? Should they assist patients in ending their own lives painlessly?

Perhaps the most controversial issues are those that implicate a Constitutional right. The Bill of Rights—the first 10 Amendments to the U.S. Constitution—spell out some of the most fundamental rights that distinguish our democracy from other nations with fewer freedoms. However, the sparsely-worded document is open to interpretation, with each side saying that the Constitution is on their side. The Bill of Rights was meant to protect individual liberties; however, the needs of some individuals clash with society's needs. Thus, the Constitution often serves as a battleground between individuals and government officials seeking to protect society in some way. The First Amendment's guarantee of "freedom of speech" leads to some very difficult questions. Some forms of expression—such as burning an American flag—lead to public outrage, but are protected by the First Amendment. Other types of expression that most people find objectionable—such as child pornography—are not protected by the Constitution. The question is not only where to draw the line, but whether drawing lines around constitutional rights threatens our liberty.

The Bill of Rights raises many other questions about individual rights and societal "good." Is a prayer before a high school football game an "establishment of religion" prohibited by the First Amendment? Does the Second Amendment's promise of "the right to bear arms" include concealed handguns? Does stopping and frisking someone standing on a known drug corner constitute "unreasonable search and seizure" in violation of the Fourth Amendment? Although the U.S. Supreme Court has the ultimate authority in interpreting the U.S. Constitution, their answers do not always satisfy the public. When a group of nine people—sometimes by a five-to-four vote—makes a decision that affects hundreds of millions of others, public outcry can be expected. For example, the Supreme Court's 1973 ruling in Roe v. Wade that abortion is protected by the Constitution did little to quell the debate over abortion.

Whatever the root of the controversy, the books in the Point-Counterpoint series seek to explain to the reader both the origins of the debate, the current state of the law, and the arguments on either side of the debate. Our hope in creating this series is that the reader will be better informed about the issues facing not only our politicians, but all of our nation's citizens, and become more actively involved in resolving these debates, as voters, concerned citizens, journalists, or maybe even elected officials.

Performance-enhancing Drugs and Sports Doping

While the Tour de France bicycle race has always been wildly popular across Europe, Americans have generally ignored the event. A scandal that swept through the race in 1998 seemed almost to guarantee that the sport of cycling would not gain equal popularity on both sides of the Atlantic. Multiple police investigations into doping led to numerous riders and entire teams being sent home. Barely half of the riders finished the multi-week race, and cycling had a well-earned reputation as a "dirty" sport.

In 1998 it seemed very unlikely that the Tour de France would capture American interest over the next decade. It seemed even less likely that Lance Armstrong would be responsible for this new interest. Less than two years earlier, after having begun to post some impressive race results, the 25-year-old Texan was diagnosed with testicular cancer that had spread to his abdomen, lungs, and brain. When he announced his diagnosis to the public, Armstrong vowed to beat the disease. He did beat it, but nobody could have predicted the magnitude of his victory.

Beginning in 1999, with cycling under a proverbial microscope, Armstrong began what might be the most astounding winning streak in the history of sports. Competing against hundreds of other riders—mostly Europeans who were not terribly interested in seeing American cyclists succeed—Armstrong powered his way through the Alps and the Pyrenees, winning the tour over seven consecutive years. Throughout his winning streak, a hostile French media, particularly the sports newspaper *L'Equipe*, tried to discredit him, printing numerous allegations of doping. Armstrong vehemently denied using performance-enhancing drugs, pointing to his consistently negative tests in the strict testing regimen that the Tour instituted after the 1998 fiasco.

When Armstrong retired following the 2005 Tour, cycling fans questioned whether Americans would retain their interest in the race. It soon seemed, however, that Armstrong had passed the torch. American Floyd Landis mounted a dramatic comeback on the day after he had a lousy ride, capturing and holding onto the yellow jersey worn by the Tour's lead rider. He kept the jersey all the way to the race's conclusion in Paris, but his triumph was short-lived. Soon after the conclusion of the race, it was announced that Landis had failed a doping test on the day of his dramatic comeback.

Landis tried to challenge his test, which showed an elevated ratio of testosterone to epitestosterone, indicative of steroid or testosterone use, but he was ridiculed in the American press for trying to come up with excuses for his positive test—including saying that he had drunk whiskey. He appealed his case before an arbitration panel of the North American Court of Arbitration for Sport and ultimately lost.

A stinging dissent by one of the arbitrators on the panel raised many questions about the way the French laboratory handled Landis's sample, and the arbitrator blasted the laboratory for leaking Landis's test results to the media. Interestingly, the same French laboratory that drew this ire also had been involved in a scandal in 2005 in which it tested long-frozen urine samples provided by Lance Armstrong, and *L'Equipe* reported the results. When questions about the ethics of laboratories are raised, situations like these make it difficult to say that anti-doping procedures are cleaning up the sport.

Types of Performance-enhancing Drugs

Some athletes use any one of a number of substances to improve their performance and gain an unfair advantage over their competitors. It is a tactic often referred to as *doping*. When people hear about doping or performance-enhancing drugs, the first things that come to mind often are steroids. Steroids include a wide variety of substances, many of which have legitimate medical uses. The type of steroid typically associated with sports doping is the anabolic steroid. These are muscle-building substances that are chemically related to testosterone. Some commonly known anabolic steroids are Deca-Durabolin, Winstrol, and nandrolone.

Testosterone is a hormone—a chemical that creates physiological responses by the human body—that occurs in both males and females, although at much higher levels in males. Because anabolic steroids are related to testosterone, they provoke some of the same physiological changes as testosterone, including muscle growth and repair. Some athletes have been caught using synthetic (laboratory-made) testosterone.

Testosterone is not the only human hormone that some athletes abuse. More recently, human growth hormone, or HGH, has gained popularity among athletes. Like testosterone, it can promote muscle growth, but unlike testosterone and steroids, it is difficult or impossible to test for HGH use.

Another class of performance-enhancing drug used by some athletes is the stimulant. Unlike steroids and hormones, which are used in training, stimulants are often used immediately

The victory for American Floyd Landis, who followed Lance Armstrong in winning the Tour de France, was short-lived. Soon after the race ended, it was announced that Landis had failed a doping test. Here, Landis testifies during an arbitration hearing on the doping allegations in May 2007.

before or during competition to improve performance on the field, court, rink, or track. Some athletes feel the drugs give them an energized feeling, allowing them to compete with intensity even when fatigued. The herbal supplement ephedra was extremely popular among athletes until the U.S. Food and Drug Administration banned it. Other stimulants with potential for athlete abuse include methamphetamine (speed) and some cold medications (when taken in large doses).

Before its ban, ephedra fell into the murky category of "dietary supplements," a hodgepodge of pills, powders, drinks, and bars that can be purchased in health food stores or on the Internet. The category includes innocuous substances like vitamins and minerals, but manufacturers can market a wide variety of substances as dietary supplements. Many of these supplements contain ingredients that are banned by sports governing

Member of Arbitration Panel Accuses French Lab of Misconduct in Landis Case

In September 2007, American cyclist Floyd Landis lost his appeal challenging a two-year ban for testing positive for an elevated testosterone-epitestosterone ratio at the 2006 Tour de France. One member of the arbitration panel disagreed strongly with the majority decision. Christopher L. Campbell concluded that Landis had been victimized by a laboratory that seemed either incompetent or intent on implicating Landis:

> From the beginning, the Laboratoire National de Dépistage et du Dopage ("LNDD") has not been trustworthy. In this case, at every stage of testing it failed to comply with the procedures and methods for testing required by the International Standards for Laboratories.... It also failed to abide by its legal and ethical obligations under the WADA Code. On the facts of this case, the LNDD should not be entrusted with Mr. Landis's career.

In his dissent, Campbell noted that the laboratory had failed to follow correct scientific procedures in running the tests, had failed to maintain a "chain of custody," or documentation of who had the sample at all times as required by WADA rules, had mislabeled Landis's sample (which was identified by a sample number bodies because they mimic the effects of steroids, hormones, or stimulants.

Another type of doping is "blood doping," or improving oxygen circulation by increasing the number of red blood cells in the blood. One method of blood doping involves having one's blood drawn long enough before a competition to allow the body to replenish the red blood cells it has left. The drawn blood is frozen, and then the red blood cells are re-injected right before competition. (Some have also used others' red blood cells or products made from blood.) An alternative method of blood doping is to use a synthetic version of the hormone erythropoietin (EPO), which generates red blood cells.

rather than by name) with the wrong sample number, and had changed dates fraudulently in documents related to the tests. Even with its sloppy work, Campbell concluded, the laboratory had failed to make a compelling case that Landis's test results even constituted a positive doping test. Furthermore, the arbitrator noted that the laboratory had breached rules by leaking the results of Landis's test to the media:

> Within 24 hours after the LNDD obtained the results, and before anyone other than the LNDD had the results, the results of the B sample tests were leaked to the media. This not only breached LNDD's obligation of confidentiality under the WADA Code, it directly violated this Panel's order. In addition to the breach of its ethical duty, the more serious aspect of the leak demonstrates LNDD's attitude towards Mr. Landis. Leaking this information was clearly meant to damage Mr. Landis's credibility before an independent tribunal had the opportunity to evaluate the evidence. This shows bias in a laboratory that should be neutral. More importantly, it shows malice. This malice brings into question everything the Laboratory has done in this case.

Source: *U.S. Anti-Doping Agency v. Landis*, AAA No. 30 190 00847 06, North American Court of Arbitration for Sport Panel, September 20, 2007 (Campbell, C.L., dissenting).

A History of Doping

The use of performance-enhancing drugs first gained attention in the United States during the 1970s. At the 1976 Olympics, East Germany, then a communist nation separated from West Germany, won twice as many medals as it had in 1972, including gold medals in 10 of the 12 individual women's events.

Years later, it would be revealed that from the late 1960s through the fall of the Berlin Wall in 1989, the East German government conducted a systematic program of doping, with many young athletes being administered steroids without their knowledge. Under the repressive regime, athletes had no choice but to participate in their sports. Many athletes later developed health problems, and some female athletes gave birth to children with severe malformations. Though the unified German government set up a system to provide a small sum of compensation to athletes who had taken part in the doping, few of those athletes claimed their money, probably to avoid media attention.

From the 1970s through the 1990s, anti-doping efforts were somewhat uneven. The International Olympic Committee, the governing bodies of individual sports, and organizing bodies from individual nations became involved in drug testing. On many fronts, however, doping proliferated.

Steroids spread to the United States, notably to the National Football League (NFL), whose athletes thought they had the most to gain from muscle-building steroids. In baseball, with its 162 games throughout the hot summer, the drug of choice was "greenies," or stimulants, which the players often turned to in order to make it through the games. Although a few players openly talked about steroids and greenies, major sports leagues effectively ignored the problems for decades. In 1986, however, NFL commissioner Pete Rozelle announced a testing policy, which would be phased in with player suspensions starting in 1989.

Major League Baseball, on the other hand, not only ignored the problem of greenies, but also allowed steroids to take over the game. With baseball losing its dominance as the nation's

Risking health and integrity to gain an unfair edge

As medical and chemical technology has developed in recent years, the international sports community has increased its efforts to combat the misuse of drugs in competition. Here are some of the drugs and methods that have been banned or restricted from Olympic competition.

Drug class	Anabolic agents	Narcotics	Peptide hormones	Blood doping	Beta blockers	Stimulants	Diuretics
Selected examples	Anabolic androgenic steroids; beta-2 agonists	Morphine; pethidine; heroin	Erythropoietin (EPO); growth hormone (hGH)	Blood infusion to boost red blood cell count	Blood pressure drugs	Amphetamines; ephedrine	Drugs that increase urine production
Reasons for misuse	Muscle growth; body fat reduction	Pain alleviation	Body fat reduction; endurance; drug-masking	Increasing oxygen capacity in blood	Preventing hands and body from shaking	Increasing alertness and aggressiveness	Weight loss; masking other drugs
Selected harmful side effects	Acne; liver, heart and psychological problems	Injury aggravation; physical dependence	Heart problems; muscle and bone damage	Infection; hypertension; immune problems	Slow heart rate; fatigue; blood vessel constriction	Physical dependence; dehydration; palpitations	Dehydration; kidney and heart problems

SOURCES: World Anti-Doping Agency; International Olympic Committee; Australian Sports Commission   AP

Though steroids are perhaps the most well known methods of enhancing performance in sports, there are many other ways to improve performance. The chart above shows several different kinds and explains the risks of each.

favorite sport, it almost seems as though the league made a conscious decision to go home run–crazy. Nobody knows for sure which baseball players were taking steroids during the 1990s because there was no drug testing, but the numbers that some players were putting up, together with the players' bulging arms, caused many to be suspicious. In 1996, Baltimore Orioles outfielder Brady Anderson, who had hit just over 70 homers in his first seven major league seasons combined, stunned the baseball world by hitting 50 in one season. He credited his use of dietary supplements such as creatine for his power surge, and no proof links him to steroid use, but that did not stop people from making allegations.

Two years later, outfielders Sammy Sosa and Mark McGwire set the baseball world on fire with a dual assault on the single-season home run record that saw both of them surpassing Roger

Maris's previous record of 61. Although both looked much bigger and more muscular than they had earlier in their careers, neither slugger was conclusively linked to steroids. But again, people were suspicious—so much so that Congress would eventually call the pair to testify. Sosa, in broken English and using an interpreter, denied using steroids, while McGwire refused to answer questions.

Anti-doping Efforts Get Serious

The year that McGwire and Sosa created such a stir was the same year that the doping scandal at the Tour de France threatened to destroy cycling. Fortunately for cycling fans, the scandal created the momentum necessary for the formation in 1999 of the World Anti-Doping Agency, or WADA, which is headquartered in Switzerland and is the ultimate watchdog of international competition. National affiliates, including the U.S. Anti-Doping Agency (USADA), test and sometimes suspend athletes.

WADA often argues for stronger penalties and can challenge national anti-doping agencies in the Court of Arbitration for Sport, also headquartered in Switzerland. The advantage of WADA and its affiliates is that it creates an independent body, with no interest in promoting any particular sport and with no national affiliation. It publishes a list of prohibited substances that is binding upon all athletes who want to participate in international competition. Critics of WADA, however, question its one-size-fits-all approach and its harsh sanctions for seemingly innocent mistakes.

WADA and USADA have no jurisdiction over professional sports leagues in the United States, although players in the National Basketball Association (NBA), National Hockey League (NHL), and Major League Baseball (MLB) who want to participate in international competitions are subject to WADA-approved testing. Since football is a uniquely American sport,

NFL players are not involved in international competition and are totally outside of WADA's authority.

Since WADA's creation, many have suggested that professional sports leagues should participate in USADA's anti-doping program, a suggestion that the leagues have resisted vehemently. In fact, it was not until congressional scrutiny in 2004 that MLB and the labor union representing its players agreed to a drug-testing program. The penalties for violating the sports' league policies are much lighter than those imposed by the World Anti-Doping Agency. WADA suspends players for two years for a first violation and gives them a lifetime ban for a second violation. On the other hand, the NFL, for example, issues a four-game suspension for a first offense and an eight-game suspension for a second offense.

Controversies Over Performance-enhancing Drugs

Listening to anti-doping advocates talk about the "scourge" of doping, or watching members of Congress denounce professional athletes for setting a bad example for the nation's youth, one would think that the consensus against performance-enhancing drugs is strong. But not everyone agrees with WADA's tactics or wants to see such strict standards extended to the NFL, the NHL, the NBA, and MLB.

It is not "politically correct" to question just how dangerous performance-enhancing drugs really are, but many people are doing just that. The dangers of steroid abuse are well documented: back acne, shrinking testicles, and emotional instability ("'roid rage"), to name a few. The medical community has a strong consensus that using steroids for athletic gain is dangerous, particularly for young people whose bodies are still growing. But some steroid users—including bodybuilders who are not subject to drug testing, and retired athletes such as Jose Canseco—say that carefully controlled steroid use by well-informed adults is worth the risk. Team owners and league officials could not make such statements without facing widespread condemnation, yet they remain willing to benefit from the athletic prowess of athletes who have used performance-enhancing drugs.

An even more delicate question is that of human growth hormone, or HGH. As professional sports leagues began testing for steroids, many athletes switched to undetectable HGH. Possessing HGH without a prescription is illegal in the United States, but many "anti-aging" clinics operate in the gray area of the law and several athletes have been linked to HGH shipments from such clinics. Nobody knows how many athletes have taken HGH, because no athlete has been tested for the hormone. It is hard to say whether the public will be as opposed to HGH use as it is regarding steroid use, given that many people who are not athletes are also using HGH.

Even to those who think that the idea of doping is bad, the methods of controlling doping raise additional issues. To many, WADA's strict controls are tantamount to a witch hunt. Anti-doping procedures are very invasive for athletes. WADA standards require athletes to keep anti-doping agencies informed of their whereabouts at all times, so that doping control agents can perform random testing at any time. Furthermore, WADA standards require that the doping control agents physically observe athletes filling urine specimen cups, and some testing procedures require athletes to provide blood samples.

The players' unions representing well-paid professional athletes are very protective of their members' generally comfortable lifestyles. They do not want them exposed to the level of intrusiveness to which international athletes are subjected. So far, players' unions have not consented to blood testing, and experts say that it might be years before a urine test for HGH is developed. Although all four major sports leagues in the United States have adopted drug-testing programs, some members of Congress are still trying to pass legislation regulating these testing programs. Opponents say that the programs already work, and that Congress has more important things to address.

Anti-doping advocates often have a difficult crusade fighting against illegal performance-enhancing drugs. When it comes to dietary supplements, the crusade is even tougher, since public sentiment is generally against treating supplements in the same way as illegal drugs. The federal government has banned some specific dietary supplements that were especially risky, but it remains legal to buy several substances that WADA and other sports governing bodies have banned. The public seemingly is tired of hearing athletes blame positive drug tests on nutritional supplements, but indeed there have been some cases in which athletes have faced long suspensions for taking supplements that they purchased legally, including multivitamins. Many athletes are unwilling to accept WADA's position that they should avoid taking any dietary supplements and must live with the consequences if they do.

Summary

Since the 1970s, fans of sports have been aware of steroid use. Once associated with bodybuilders and Olympic athletes from communist countries, steroids have crept into almost every sport. Athletes have turned to other performance-enhancing drugs, including hormones, stimulants, and steroid-like dietary supplements, to gain an edge—or, some say, simply to keep up with the competition.

The American public has mixed feelings about steroids. Many watch in delight when athletes surrounded by doping allegations perform astounding feats. Most Americans are not sure that the government should be involved in anti-doping efforts, at least as far as adult professional athletes are concerned. Few stand in the way of efforts to rid high school and college sports of performance-enhancing drugs. The question of regulating doping in the four major sports leagues—the NFL, the NHL, the NBA, and MLB—is much more controversial, even though these leagues have lagged behind Olympic sports in their drug-testing policies. Complicating the effort to rid sports of doping is a multibillion-dollar dietary supplement industry, which has strong allies in Congress who fight any effort to tighten restrictions on muscle-building supplements.

The Media Has Blown the "Problem" of Performance-enhancing Drugs out of Proportion

If ever there was an athlete whom one would expect to be unanimously voted into the Baseball Hall of Fame, it is baseball's "iron man," Cal Ripken Jr. During his career, in which he was named an All-Star player 19 times, he distinguished himself both for his defensive play at shortstop and for his hitting, collecting more than 400 home runs and more than 3,000 hits. He is best known, however, for his record for most consecutive games played, surpassing Lou Gehrig's old record of 2,130 by more than 500 additional games.

Off the field, Ripken was beloved by the city of Baltimore, where he played his entire career. He has always had a squeaky-clean image as a family man, and today as a "sports ambassador" for the U.S. government, promoting American sports overseas. He has given millions to support youth baseball and has also been prominent in raising money to cure ALS—also called Lou Gehrig's disease—a debilitating and fatal disorder.

Yet, when it came time for Chicago sportswriter Paul Ledewski to submit his ballot for the Baseball Hall of Fame, Ledewski refused to cast a vote for Ripken or any of the other candidates on the 2007 ballot. His rationale? Ripken played during a time when Major League Baseball did not have a strict steroids policy, and in Ledewski's mind, that tainted the records of everyone who played the game. In explaining his refusal to vote, he wrote: "I don't have nearly enough information to make a value judgment of this magnitude [concerning] any player in the Steroids Era, which I consider to be the 1993 to 2004 period, give or a take a season."[1]

Ledewski took this course of action even though nothing suggested to him that either Ripken or fellow first-time candidate Tony Gwynn, one of the most reliable hitters of all time, were taking steroids. Rather, he took a "guilty until proven innocent" approach:

> This isn't to suggest that Gwynn or Ripken or the majority of the other eligible candidates padded his statistics with performance-enhancers and cheated the game, their predecessors and the fans in the process. . . . But tell me, except for the players themselves, who can say what they put into their bodies over the years with any degree of certainty?[2]

Although Ledewski's actions were extreme and drew criticism from fellow sportswriters, he was, many would say, reflective of an overly eager media industry that has blown the "steroid problem" out of proportion. In these days of 24-hour news coverage, media professionals are scrambling to fill airtime on daily radio and television shows, and space in blogs, newspaper columns, and magazine articles. A byproduct of this is sensationalist coverage of some topics and events, including, critics say, the issue of performance-enhancing drugs.

Sports governing bodies have done an adequate job of addressing substance use.

Fueling the fire of media sensationalism about steroids are comments speculating about the widespread nature of steroids and other performance-enhancing drugs in sports. These comments often come from interest groups, opportunistic politicians, and former athletes looking for attention. For example, former outfielder Jose Canseco showed up uninvited at the news conference unveiling the Mitchell Report (a report on steroid use in baseball produced by former U.S. senator George Mitchell), likely in an effort to promote a new book. Another player alleges that Canseco threatened to implicate him in steroid use if he did not back Canseco's movie project.

Dick Pound, former chairman of WADA, is a frequent critic of sports leagues and has made allegations that the use of performance-enhancing drugs is widespread even in leagues with a drug-testing policy. For example, in 2005, Pound told a Canadian newspaper that he believed that one-third of players in the National Hockey League (NHL) were using performance-enhancing drugs.[3] The NHL office and players' union responded swiftly and angrily to Pound's accusations. The league's deputy commissioner Bill Daly said Pound's comments "have absolutely no basis in fact," while players' union head Ted Saskin said, "He has no knowledge of our sport and our players and frankly has no business making such comments."[4]

At the time Pound made his comments, the league had just adopted its first-ever testing program for performance-enhancing drugs. The league's actions appear to be based on public and political pressure rather than the need for testing. Earlier, NHL commissioner Gary Bettman had testified before a Senate subcommittee that, unlike some other sports, hockey is not a sport in which players feel pressure to use performance-enhancing drugs. According to Bettman's testimony:

> In the experience of the doctors who administer our program, the primary alleged benefit of steroid use, significant

large muscle development, is not consistent with playing our sport at the highest levels. The bulkiness attributable to steroid use simply is not a desired characteristic of NHL players. To the extent there might be some limited usage of performance-enhancing substances in the NHL, we believe that our program will eradicate any such use.[5]

Nevertheless, the league had negotiated a drug-testing policy in the 2005 collective bargaining agreement with the players' union. According to Bettman, the primary benefit in the testing program is not necessarily the reduction of drug use, but the maintenance of fan confidence in the sport:

> While it is the league's firm belief that the performance-enhancing drug issue is not a problem in the NHL, the league is committed to providing its fans with outstanding athletic competition with the assurance that our game is being conducted in an environment free of performance-enhancing substances.[6]

In the years after the NHL instituted its steroid testing policy, Bettman's suggestions seem to have been borne out by test results. As of the start of 2008, only one player, defenseman Sean Hill, has failed an NHL drug test, while two other NHL players failed tests administered to potential members of Olympic teams. Defenseman Bryan Berard tested positive for a steroid in a test administered to potential members of the U.S. Olympic team, while goaltender Jose Theodore raised eyebrows around the league with a positive test for finasteride in a test administered to potential members of the Canadian national team. Steroid users can use this substance to mask steroid use, and it is therefore on the banned list for Olympic athletes. However, finasteride is also the active ingredient in the hair-loss drug Propecia, and Theodore publicly announced that he was taking the drug to keep his hair looking good. It was hard to say which was more improbable—that the shaggy-haired Theodore would need a hair-loss drug, or that a slender goalie protected from game contact by the referees would need steroids.

The risks of steroids and other performance-enhancing drugs are overstated.

In his book *Juiced*, retired slugger Jose Canseco credited steroids for much of his success in Major League Baseball and denied ever having any steroid-related health problems. Reflecting on how good he felt at age 40, he asked rhetorically, "If I were exaggerating the effect that growth hormone and steroids can have when used properly and carefully as part of a program of weight lifting, fitness, careful nutrition, and clean living, then why would I look and feel as good as I do?"[7]

Although organizations such as the NCAA and International Olympic Committee, as well as the U.S. government, have extensive campaigns warning young people of the danger of steroids, a few experts have departed from the "company line" to challenge the notion that steroids are universally dangerous.

For years, the face of the battle against steroid use was that of a dying Lyle Alzado. The once-fierce defensive lineman known for his wild on-field antics was diagnosed with brain cancer. He gave numerous interviews in which he acknowledged that he had begun using steroids in college and used them throughout his pro career. He warned others not to follow his example. Brain cancer, however, is not one of the risks typically associated with steroid use. In a biography for ESPN, Mike Puma writes, "Although there is no medical link between steroids and brain lymphoma, Alzado was certain the drugs were responsible for his cancer. He became a symbol of the dangers of steroid abuse."[8]

Standing in the midst of the medical community's warnings against the use of performance-enhancing drugs, there is physiologist Jose Antonio. The CEO of the International Society of Sports Nutrition, Antonio is one of the leading voices in challenging across-the-board criticisms of steroid use. He has authored or coauthored several articles that discount the dangers. For example, in an article published by the *Canadian Journal of Applied Physiology*, he and two colleagues reviewed published scientific research about the effects of steroids. They concluded:

> Although androgens have been available to athletes for over 50 years, there is little evidence to show that their use will cause any long-term detriment; furthermore, the use of moderate doses of androgens results in side effects that are largely benign and reversible. It is our contention that the incidence of serious health problems associated with the use of androgens by athletes has been overstated.[9]

In a later study, Antonio and colleagues gave both low and high doses of two steroids to healthy male athletes. The researchers administered standard drug tests to see if the athletes would test positive, and also monitored the effects of the steroids on the kidney, liver, blood, and immune system. The study concluded, "All subjects tested positive via urinalysis for the presence of nortestosterone at days 3, 5, 7, and 10. . . . Furthermore . . . there was no effect on renal, hepatic, hematological, or bone marrow function. Thus, short-term ingestion of [the two steroids] may result in a positive drug test result without any harmful side effects."[10]

In an article entitled "Pumped-Up Hysteria," appearing in the libertarian magazine *Reason*, baseball writer Dayn Perry argued that steroid use could not be conclusively blamed for various problems such as aggressive behavior, liver cancer, heart disease, high blood pressure, or high cholesterol. He concludes: "In short, steroids are a significant threat to neither the health of the players nor the health of the game [of baseball]. Yet the country has returned to panic mode, with both private and public authorities declaring war on tissue-building drugs."[11]

Critics of steroid bans are careful, however, to point out that they are making their arguments about healthy professional athletes who have information about how to use steroids safely. "If you abuse steroids, they can be very harmful," Canseco warns. "That's why using them only in a careful, controlled way is so important. It takes education, personal discipline, and common sense."[12] The health risks to younger people, those with health problems, and those who use steroids improperly can be very real. Even in preaching the virtues of steroids, Canseco warns against their use by people whose bodies are still developing.

The popularity of athletic competition is at an all-time high.

According to many sportswriters and fan bloggers, steroid users and users of other performance-enhancing drugs undermine fan interest in sports. But although poll numbers often show public disapproval of steroid use, this disapproval has not translated into a lack of fan interest. If anything, fan interest in sports is at an all-time high, despite investigations linking high-profile athletes to performance-enhancing drugs.

In fact, the performance of several prominent sluggers dogged by steroid accusations—including Sammy Sosa, Mark McGwire, and Barry Bonds—has increased fan interest in baseball. When Sosa and McGwire began chasing baseball's single-season record for home runs, the sport had still not rebounded from a player strike in 1994. During the 1998 season, in which both players surpassed the decades-old mark of 61 home runs and McGwire finished with 70, attendance around the league surged. Overall, attendance was up more than 7 million, an increase of more than 10 percent from the previous year, and total attendance topped 70 million for the first time.

As Barry Bonds continued his assault on the record book, attendance continued to soar. In the early years of the new millennium, MLB continued to set league-wide attendance records, surpassing 75 million fans for the first time in 2006. Bonds broke not only the record for home runs in a single season, but also surpassed Hank Aaron to be baseball's all-time home run king. During his countdown toward the record, many criticized Bonds, who was the subject of the book *Game of Shadows*, which alleged his long-term steroid use. Fans, however, continued to show great interest in Bonds's achievements. Although steroid use (or alleged steroid use) has its critics, fans are still enjoying the sports that are under so much scrutiny by politicians and the media.

Drug-testing procedures are unnecessarily invasive.

Although members of Congress have called on the major sports leagues (MLB, the NBA, the NFL, and the NHL) to step up testing of athletes and use more accurate testing, the leagues and their players' associations have taken the position that they are already doing a great deal of testing. They argue that stepping up testing efforts would be an administrative burden and an undue interference with athletes' lives.

In 2005, Senator Frank Lautenberg called the representatives of the four major sports leagues and their players' unions to testify before Congress. In doing so, he sent written questions to each league, including an inquiry regarding whether Congress should impose uniform drug-testing requirements on all sports leagues.

NBA commissioner David Stern's response was influenced by calls from WADA and certain politicians for more frequent testing, both in-season and during the off-season. He wrote to Senator Lautenberg:

> Some leagues (such as the NBA) have longer seasons than others, making off-season testing less important. Some leagues play games every day; some only play once a week. Each individual league needs the flexibility to design a drug policy and testing program that is correctly tailored to its unique circumstances.[13]

Deputy commissioner Bill Daly of the NHL noted that only 8 hockey players out of 3,000 tested for international competition had ever tested positive. Daly said he felt that increased drug testing was not necessary in his league:

> The applicable standards would need to recognize and reflect the practicalities and legalities that would arise from mandatory off-season testing of NHL players, given that our players come from twenty-two (22) countries across the globe, and eighty-five (85) percent of our players come from outside the United States, many of whom return to their country of origin during the off-season. Other sports simply may not need to address these circumstances. In addition, while it may be appropriate to spend the financial resources necessary to test players five (5) times during the calendar year in a sport that has a suspected or confirmed history of performance-enhancing drug use, it may not be necessary or appropriate to do so in a sport such as hockey which has no such historical experience.[14]

In his queries, Senator Lautenberg also asked the leagues' officials why they did not conduct blood tests for performance-enhancing drugs. At the time, the Olympics planned to test athletes for HGH at the upcoming 2006 games, using a blood test that had not yet been widely accepted by the scientific community. Daly argued that the administration of blood tests to NHL athletes in a widespread manner was an extreme and unwarranted step:

> First, we have not seen scientific evidence that the blood tests currently administered do, in fact, materially enhance the ability to accurately and reliably detect substances such as the human growth hormone. Second, we believe that administering 3,500 blood tests annually (five tests per player for 700 NHL players) would be excessively invasive, costly, and

time-consuming. Notably, WADA will conduct a total of only 88 in-competition blood tests during the 2006 Olympic Games, which involve numerous different competitions and many hundreds of athletes. To the extent blood tests are used at all outside of the context of international athletic competitions, we believe it is similarly appropriate to do so only in very limited circumstances.[15]

With fewer positive steroids tests among NFL players, speculation about their use of human growth hormone (HGH) increased when several athletes were linked to investigations of illegal distribution of HGH. New England Patriots defensive back Rodney Harrison was suspended for four games in the 2007 season, reportedly because he had been linked to an HGH source. Later, as the Patriots prepared for the Super Bowl, reporters at a Super Bowl press conference asked Gene Upshaw, president of the NFL Players' Association, about HGH testing. The union boss replied that the league would consider it, but that they maintained their opposition to blood tests: "Until a test is developed for HGH, there's really not an awful lot to talk about. And when that test is developed, we really believe it should be a urine test. No one is interested in a blood test. We got a lot of big, tough guys, but they don't even like to be pricked on the finger to give blood."[16]

Because substances such as HGH are currently undetectable, and because labs such as BALCO have produced "designer" steroids for which tests are not yet employed, some testing proponents favor freezing blood or urine samples for later testing. Freezing urine samples is common practice in cycling, which has seen numerous doping scandals over the years. In 2005, the French sporting newspaper *L'Equipe* reported that the French National Laboratory had unfrozen and tested six urine samples collected from seven-time Tour de France champion Lance Armstrong in 1999, during the first of his tour victories. The

Cyclist Lance Armstrong is shown before a training ride in May 1998, the year before he won his first Tour de France. In 2005, French sporting newspaper *L'Equipe* reported that six urine samples collected from Armstrong in 1999 had tested positive for EPO, a performance-enhancing substance.

publication announced that the samples tested positive for EPO, a performance-enhancing substance for which testing had not yet been developed in 1999.

Armstrong disputed the claims, and no official action was taken against him. Still, his reputation was damaged, having been once again cast in a negative light by a French press eager to bring down an American who had dominated a traditionally European sport. Although Armstrong never failed a doping test during his career, he was forced to continually answer doping allegations after bouncing back from testicular cancer to dominate the sport's most prominent event. In the case of the unfrozen samples, Armstrong had no way to defend himself, as these were backup samples. No additional samples remained to be tested in a manner in which Armstrong's representatives could ensure the absence of bias or faulty methodologies.

Freezing and storing blood and urine raises many questions. In the case of the testing of Armstrong's samples, it appears that testing can be done in an effort to discredit a single athlete, and the testing raised questions about whether proper procedures were followed. Additionally, one can gather information from blood and urine samples that could be used for other purposes. For example, could blood samples taken from athletes be entered into the DNA database maintained by the Federal Bureau of Investigation (FBI) for investigating unsolved crimes? Could a lab storing an athlete's frozen blood be forced to turn over a sample in a paternity case? Testing outside of a one-time urinalysis raises many ethical questions, and the players' unions of the major professional sports leagues have acted to protect their members' privacy.

These privacy concerns are more than just theoretical. During investigations into the steroid company BALCO, the federal government seized computer records from Comprehensive Drug Testing, Inc., a company hired to perform what Major League Baseball players had been assured would be anonymous tests. A federal appeals court upheld the seizure of the computer records, noting:

> The government was not required to believe, and had no reason to assume, that all relevant documents in the [database] would be listed under the names of the baseball players in the warrant. The government's decision to copy the entire directory represented a conscientious effort to seek out all the evidence covered by the search warrant. We do not discern bad faith or "callous disregard" simply because the agents determined, after an initial review, that certain inter-mingled files needed to be reviewed off site. . . .[17]

The records seized with the court's approval contained medical information about every MLB player and numerous other athletes, even though the government only had a warrant to

Federal Judge Blasts Seizure of Thousands of Test Results Without Grounds for Suspicion

As part of the BALCO probe, the federal government obtained a warrant to seize the test results of 11 baseball players implicated in performance-enhancing drug use. In addition to the records of those 11 players, law enforcement officials also seized computer records with the drug-test results of every MLB player and many other athletes. The lower court ruled that the seizure violated the Fourth Amendment, but a federal appeals court overturned the lower court. One of the judges on the appeals court dissented from the majority ruling:

> One of the three extremely able district court judges who rejected the government's argument summarized it best, stating: "What happened to the Fourth Amendment? Was it repealed somehow?"
>
> Although it only had a search warrant for data concerning 11 Major League Baseball players, the government seized thousands of medical records and test results involving every single Major League Baseball player. The government did not stop there, seizing thousands of other medical records for individuals in 13 other major sports organizations, 3 unaffiliated business entities, and 3 sports competitions. The government now seeks to retain all of the medical information it obtained about persons who were not the subject of any criminal inquiry.
>
> The stakes in this case are high. The government claims the right to search—without warrant or even a suspicion of criminal activity—any patient's confidential medical record contained in a computer directory so long as it has a legitimate warrant or subpoena for any other individual patient's record that may be contained as part of data stored on the same computer. The government attempts to justify this novel theory on a breathtaking expansion of the "plain view" doctrine, which clearly has no application to intermingled private electronic data.

Source: *U.S. v. Comprehensive Drug Testing*, 473 F.3d 915 (9th Cir. 2006) (Thomas, J., dissenting).

gather information about 11 players implicated in the BALCO probe.

Summary

The media has dedicated extensive and provocative coverage to the use of performance-enhancing drugs by high-profile athletes. There is much speculation that the use of performance-enhancing drugs is widespread, or even universal, among professional athletes in leagues with less stringent testing policies than those athletes employed in international competition. Even Congress has gotten involved, calling league officials and some sports superstars to testify.

The leagues and their players' unions maintain that the allegations have been blown out of proportion. They deny that steroid use has in any way diminished the integrity of athletic competition, and they point out that interest in athletics remains high. Additionally, even some scientists question whether steroids are as harmful as they are made out to be. Representatives of MLB, the NFL, the NBA, the NHL, and their players' unions do not favor more invasive testing, such as blood testing or storing samples for future use.

Performance-enhancing Drugs Are Damaging the Integrity of Athletic Competition

On August 7, 2007, San Francisco Giants outfielder Barry Bonds hit his 756th career home run, breaking the all-time record held for three decades by Hank Aaron. The contrast between the two sluggers was startling. Aaron, despite being the all-time king of home runs, had never hit 50 homers in a single season and was one of the most consistent hitters in league history, piling up numbers year after year. Bonds, by contrast, had a massive power surge late in his career.

Rail-thin while playing for the Pittsburgh Pirates, Bonds was considered a complete player, who could get on base, steal bases, and hit for power. Later in his career, while with the Giants, Bonds went through some well-documented changes. While his base stealing tailed off, his power went through the roof. No longer the wiry player who played for the Pirates, everything about him seemed huge: His arms, his legs, his chest, and even his head seemed gigantic. Around the league, people began to whisper about steroids. When Bonds hit 73 home runs in 2001, breaking Mark McGwire's record, people talked about whether Bonds would have an asterisk next to the total. (Baseball had for years put an asterisk next to Roger Maris's record of 61, recognizing that he hit those home runs in a 162-game season, while Babe Ruth had hit 60 in only 154 games.)

In 2003, Bonds's doubters finally got some evidence of what they had expected. Federal agents raided BALCO labs in northern California, after a long investigation in which they seized illegal performance-enhancing drugs and records tying numerous high-profile athletes to a doping regimen overseen by BALCO. Evidence linked both Bonds and his trainer, Greg Anderson, to BALCO. They were specifically linked to two substances: "The Clear," a new steroid for which athletes were not yet being tested, and "The Cream," a substance that protected athletes from testing positive for an elevated testosterone-to-epitestosterone ratio (a standard anti-doping test). The lead investigator claims that

National Labor Relations Act, 29 U.S.C., sections 151–169

Congress has criticized players' unions, particularly the MLBPA, for standing in the way of more comprehensive drug testing. Federal law, however, gives athletes the right to form unions and collectively bargain with the leagues regarding working conditions. The National Labor Relations Act (NLRA) states:

Employees shall have the right to self-organization, to form, join, or assist labor organizations, to bargain collectively through representatives of their own choosing, and to engage in other concerted activities for the purpose of collective bargaining or other mutual aid or protection....

Source: 29 U.S.C., sec. 157.

BALCO founder Victor Conte admitted to him that Bonds was receiving these substances, although Conte later recanted the story.

A grand jury was convened to prosecute BALCO's ringleaders, and the government called a number of high-profile athletes to appear as witnesses. Though the proceedings were to remain secret, investigative reporters Mark Fainaru-Wada and Lance Williams detailed leaked testimony in their book *Game of Shadows*. While a number of athletes admitted to steroid use in order to avoid prosecution, Bonds denied knowingly using steroids, instead claiming that Anderson had given him flaxseed oil and arthritic balm.

In their book, Fainaru-Wada and Williams spell out a case that Bonds's late-career renaissance was what it seemed—too good to be true. They write: "Of the four best seasons in Bonds's career, four came after he was 35 years old—and after 1999, the year he began using steroids."[18] In 2007, federal authorities charged Bonds with perjury, and the Giants announced that Bonds would not be in a Giants uniform in 2008.

Ironically, most people feel that Bonds could have been in the Hall of Fame regardless of whether he used steroids, as Fainaru-Wada and Williams allege he did in 1999. Whether or not Bonds ever faces criminal penalties or discipline by Major League Baseball, his legacy has been tarnished. The young man who retrieved the ball hit by Bonds for his 756th home run sold it to fashion designer Mark Ecko, who, after paying hundreds of thousands of dollars for the ball, asked the public what to do with it. He ended up marking the ball itself with an asterisk.

The use of performance-enhancing drugs is pervasive in professional sports leagues and international competition.

Depending on the sport and the level of competition, drug-testing procedures range from strict to almost nonexistent. In Olympic competition, for example, athletes are tested frequently, without warning, both during competition and during the off-season. Major professional sports leagues in the United States differ. First, testing in U.S. sports is typically done only during the sport's season, and several athletes have spoken out to say that they receive some sort of warning before a "random" test is administered. Second, although blood testing is used in some sports, the major sports leagues in the United States use urine testing only. Third, in Olympic and international competition, athletes are tested for a broad range of substances, while in U.S. sports leagues, athletes are tested for a more limited range of substances agreed to in collective bargaining between the league and the players' union.

While testing in professional baseball, basketball, football, and hockey has become more stringent over the past decade, athletes in these sports continue to try to beat the tests. In a story for ESPN.com, investigative reporter Mike Fish detailed pervasive steroid use among baseball prospects in the Dominican Republic. He cited statistics provided by Major League Baseball that of the first 289 players in major, minor, and summer leagues to test positive for performance-enhancing drugs, 169 were from the Dominican Republic—nearly 60 percent.[19]

Analyzing the problem, Fish notes that the Dominican Republic is a poor country that, for a small island nation, has produced a large number of major leaguers. Watching these local heroes in action and getting a glimpse of their extravagant lifestyle leads many young Dominicans to aspire to play baseball professionally. Adult Dominicans have also seen opportunity in Major League Baseball: Because Dominicans are not subject to a league draft as U.S. players are, Dominican teens can sign with the highest bidder. Entrepreneurs have formed baseball "academies" to train young players, who later pay a commission to the academy if they sign a professional contract. Fish describes the success of this model:

> The investment in that teenage talent has grown to the point
> that MLB officials estimate the Dominican Republic is home

to more than 6,000 independent baseball academies, each typically grooming a dozen or so players who may potentially sign pro contracts. They're fed and housed at the academies, then, once they're signed by teams, the people running the camps take a cut of the bonus.[20]

According to Fish, the model is successful in funneling Dominican youths into American baseball, but it also creates an incentive to cheat. Although the baseball academies stand to lose money if a player tests positive after signing, Fish detailed allegations that some of the academies might be pressuring youths into taking steroids in order to impress professional talent scouts.

It is not just aspiring athletes who are affected by the pressure created by steroids. Unfortunately, as the use of performance-enhancing drugs creeps into athletic competition, athletes face a dilemma: use the drugs, or else lose to those who do. Frank Shorter, former Olympic marathoner, testified before Congress in 2002 on behalf of the U.S. Anti-Doping Association. In his testimony, he gave a personal perspective on how steroids destroy the spirit of competition, recalling the unfairness of a concerted effort by East Germany to use steroids to dominate the Olympics during the early 1970s:

> I won the gold medal for the United States in the marathon in the 1972 Olympics in Munich. And four years later, I ran an even better race, but finished second to an East German at the Montreal games. At the time, I knew it would be absolutely possible to increase my performances and increase my chances of beating the East Germans and others who were using steroids—and let me tell you, the athletes know who's doing what—but it never occurred to me to do so. To me, that's not what sport is about. I didn't cheat, and I finished second.[21]

Some sports have been particularly notorious for the use of performance-enhancing drugs and other tactics such as blood doping. Professional cycling has seen more than its share of scandals. The 1998 Tour de France, for instance, was marred by doping scandals even before the cyclists lined up at the starting line. A masseur from the Festina team was arrested with a large supply of doping products and equipment, which he later admitted was for team use. Police searched the hotel of a second team, TVM, and the riders of that team were detained by police and subjected to extensive drug testing. The tour's other riders, protesting what they perceived to be unfair treatment of the TVM riders, staged sit-downs that delayed the tour. Several teams and individual riders also dropped out of the tour, with only 14 of the original 21 teams remaining and just over half of the tour's 189 riders crossing the finish line.

Anabolic Steroid Control Act of 2004

Reacting to the spike in sales of androstenedione ("andro") and the use by elite athletes of the "designer" steroid tetrahydrogestrinone (THG, also known as "the clear") to avoid current testing procedures, Congress passed a law broadening the definition of anabolic steroids banned under federal law. In addition to banning andro, THG, and numerous substances by name, the act banned:

> any drug or hormonal substance, chemically and pharmacologically related to testosterone (other than estrogens, progestins, corticosteroids, and dehydroepiandrosterone), and includes ... any salt, ester, or ether of a drug or substance described in this paragraph.

The exclusion of dehydroepiandrosterone, or DHEA (not to be confused with "DSHEA," the dietary supplement law), was controversial. Senator Orrin Hatch of Utah, a state that is home to many supplement makers, insisted that DHEA be excluded from the act, even though most sports governing bodies had banned it and many consider it to be a steroid precursor rather than a legitimate dietary supplement.

Source: Anabolic Steroid Control Act of 2004, Pub. L. no. 108–358, 108th Congress, 2d session (2004).

Professional cycling has responded aggressively to wide-spread doping and has instituted strict and frequent testing. Nevertheless, the use of performance-enhancing drugs has not disappeared from the sport, leading many to question the sport's legitimacy. WADA sent independent observers to the 2003 Tour de France to examine and report on the new testing procedures put into place that year. Riders received blood tests before the race started, and at each stage, riders were subjected to random drug testing, as were the winner of each stage and the overall leader of the multiweek tour.

Most sports governing bodies have not done enough, and players' unions have hampered efforts.

Although the Tour de France performed daily testing, the WADA observers found fault with the procedures. Tour officials did not wait until each stage's conclusion to announce who would be tested at random. Instead, they made the announcement five minutes before the start of the first stage and then 20 minutes prior to the end of each of the subsequent stages. The WADA observers concluded:

> [During the first stage] the cyclists who were not notified then still had the opportunity to take a stimulant before the start of the race, as they were certain not to be tested (unless they won!) . . . [During the road stages] the riders who were not selected again had an opportunity to take a fast-acting stimulant because they knew for certain they would not be tested (unless they won!)[22]

Additionally, riders had one hour to report for testing after finishing each stage and were not observed during that time. The WADA observers recommended the following: "Once notification has been given, an escort trained specially for this purpose should accompany the rider until he arrives at the anti-doping control station." They also recommended that the rider should have only 30 minutes to report for testing, with an additional 20 minutes granted if he needed to attend a press conference.[23] If WADA needed ammunition to back up its claims that cycling had not rid itself of doping, the stripping of the 2006 championship from Floyd Landis for a failed drug test once again cast a shadow over the sport.

Other sports that have instituted supposedly strict testing procedures also have been a step behind the cheaters. Among U.S. professional sports leagues, the NFL has been at the forefront of steroid testing after allegations of steroid use began to mar the sport's reputation. However, as sportswriter Shaun Assael notes in his book *Steroid Nation*, despite the league's "reputation as a dedicated partner in the doping fight," the league still experiences problems.[24] "On any given Sunday, a good portion of the league was still probably hopped up on something," Assael writes. "Unlike in baseball, where muscle enhancement was a matter of will and greed, in the NFL where super-sized men collided at supernatural speeds, it was a matter of survival."[25]

With men weighing more than 300 pounds running around the field, the NFL has obvious reasons to be vigilant about performance-enhancing drugs. Athletes in almost any sport can benefit professionally from drug use, though, and the other professional leagues have demonstrated an almost willing indifference to drug use.

Former Major League Baseball slugger Jose Canseco is one of the few professional athletes to openly acknowledge steroid use. In fact, he wrote a book, *Juiced*, detailing his own steroid use and alleging that other major leaguers used steroids. Testifying before Congress, Canseco alleged that 80 percent of MLB players were using steroids at the peak of steroid use, which he placed at sometime between 1994 and 2000.[26] He also said the league and its teams did nothing to stop the use. Canseco charged that, rather than acting upon an obvious problem, the league instead tried to discredit those who, like Canseco, spoke out about the depth of the problem: "Because of my truthful revelations I have had to endure attacks on my credibility. . . . All of these attacks have been spurred on by an organization that holds itself above the law. An organization that chose to exploit its players for the increased revenue that lines its pockets. . . ."[27]

Part of the problem with drug testing initiated by the sports leagues is that each of the leagues has collective bargaining agreements with the labor unions representing the players. Under federal law, workers have the right to organize themselves into labor unions. They can bargain not only for financial issues such as salary, retirement pensions, health insurance, and guarantees of being paid even when injured, but also for working conditions such as drug-testing procedures and the length of training camp. Prior to 2002, the MLB Players' Association remained opposed to random drug testing of its members.

Labor laws were originally designed to protect factory workers who toiled in unsafe conditions for pennies a day. Some have questioned directly whether labor laws were ever intended to protect millionaire athletes from being tested for drugs that are illegal under federal law and directly impact the way they perform their jobs. Before MLB adopted its often-criticized testing policy, Senator Peter Fitzgerald went on the offensive against Donald Fehr, the chief of the MLB Players' Association. Fitzgerald asked Fehr during a Congressional hearing:

> Do you think members of your union, now that they see the Senate holding hearings on this, understand that, if they were to oppose mandatory drug testing, that they could be inviting congressional action that would probably be more draconian than a voluntary program or an internal agreement amongst the players and owners in Major League Baseball? Are the players aware that they could have the force of law requiring some kind of mandatory testing?[28]

Fitzgerald's point was well taken by the players' union, and they agreed to drug testing in their next collective bargaining agreement. Under the terms of the agreement, players would be tested anonymously, and if more than 5 percent tested positive, then the league would begin random testing with penalties for those players who tested positive. Under the agreement, there was no suspension for a first-time drug offense. In 2003, more than 5 percent of players tested positive, triggering the random tests. The policy was modified twice in 2005, first to add HGH to the list of banned substances and provide for a 10-game suspension for a first offense, and then later to increase the first-offense suspension to 50 games, with 100-game bans for repeat offenders and a lifetime ban for a "third strike."

The testing program, however, has been the subject of widespread criticism, particularly by those who note the differences between WADA's rules governing international competition and the rules adopted by MLB. With controversy swirling around Barry Bonds and other players, baseball commissioner Bud Selig asked former U.S. Senator George Mitchell, who had several ties to baseball, to conduct an investigation of performance-enhancing drugs in the sport. Mitchell's report found that the current testing policy made it possible for players to continue to use performance-enhancing drugs.

One problem noted by Mitchell was that the players were not subjected to a sufficient number of unannounced tests throughout the season and off-season. Mitchell discussed allegations that players knew when they were to be tested during the 2003 and 2004 seasons, but he was not able to determine the truth of those allegations. Regardless, Mitchell felt that MLB needed more random testing if it was to tackle the problem head-on:

> Adequate year-round, unannounced testing is essential to any effective drug-testing program. While strong sanctions for violators are necessary, those sanctions are meaningless unless testing maximizes the chance that violators will be

detected. If tests are limited, predictable, or announced in advance, players can avoid detection and evade discipline.[29]

Furthermore, Mitchell found that the testing program had simply caused players to shift to performance-enhancing drugs that were either not yet banned or could not be detected by tests. The report found: "The current program has been effective in that detectable steroid use appears to have declined. However, that does not mean that players have stopped using performance-enhancing substances. Many players have shifted to human growth hormone, which is not detectable in any currently available urine test."[30]

Given the deficiency of testing methods, Mitchell urged MLB officials to use traditional investigative methods to detect drug use. For example, athletes including outfielder Gary Matthews Jr., as well as high-profile athletes in other sports, had been linked to human growth hormone during the investigation of a Florida company distributing HGH through the mail. Mitchell suggested that MLB needed a separate investigations department because the current league structure placed too much emphasis on maintaining good relationships with players and not enough emphasis on ending rule violations. He concluded:

> The [labor relations] department must maintain good relations with the Players Association; but aggressive, thorough investigations of the alleged possession or use by players of performance-enhancing substances may be inconsistent with that objective. Many of the investigations involving performance-enhancing substances have not been aggressive or thorough. Before this investigation, with few exceptions, the Commissioner's Office had not conducted investigative interviews of current major league players regarding alleged possession or use of performance-enhancing substances, by that player or by others. . . .[31]

Additionally, he said:

> The Commissioner should create a Department of Investigations, led by a senior executive who reports directly to the president of Major League Baseball. Ideally, this senior executive should have experience as a senior leader in law enforcement, with the highest credibility among state and federal law enforcement officials; the success of this department will depend in part upon how well it interacts with law enforcement authorities. The senior executive should have sole authority over all investigations of alleged performance-enhancing substance violations and other threats to the integrity of the game, and should receive the resources and other support needed to make the office effective.[32]

Steroids and other performance-enhancing drugs are dangerous.

Many of the substances taken by athletes as performance-enhancing drugs have legitimate medical purposes. For example, anabolic steroids are sometimes prescribed by doctors to cancer or surgery patients or people with endocrine, skin, or blood disorders. The FDA has approved human growth hormone for the treatment of hormone deficiencies in children who are not growing, people with certain genetic and kidney disorders, and AIDS patients suffering from muscle wasting. The use of HGH as an "anti-aging" medication is more controversial, with some doctors prescribing HGH to wealthy clients who want to stall the natural effects of aging.

When doctors use these substances for legitimate medical purposes, they are carefully controlling the dosages, monitoring the effects on the body, and most importantly, weighing the benefits of treatment against the risks of using the substances. Because athletic competition has taken place for thousands of years without these substances, one would argue that there is no

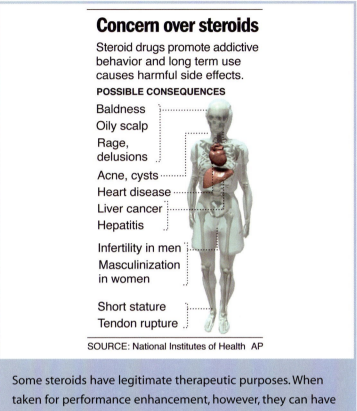

Concern over steroids

Steroid drugs promote addictive behavior and long term use causes harmful side effects.

POSSIBLE CONSEQUENCES

Baldness
Oily scalp
Rage, delusions
Acne, cysts
Heart disease
Liver cancer
Hepatitis
Infertility in men
Masculinization in women
Short stature
Tendon rupture

SOURCE: National Institutes of Health AP

Some steroids have legitimate therapeutic purposes. When taken for performance enhancement, however, they can have negative side effects, as detailed in the graphic above.

legitimate benefit to their use as performance enhancers, and that therefore only the risks remain.

The U.S. Drug Enforcement Agency (DEA) is taking a more aggressive approach to warning people about the illegality and risks of performance-enhancing drugs. For example, the agency's March 2004 pamphlet warns of certain risks of steroid use, including the following:

- High blood cholesterol levels, which may lead to cardiovascular problems;

- Thinning of hair and baldness;

- High blood pressure;

- Liver disorders (liver damage and jaundice);

- Harm to fetal development during pregnancy;

- Risk of contracting HIV and other blood-borne diseases from sharing infected needles;

- Sexual and reproductive disorders in males: a wasting away of the testicles, loss of sexual drive, decreased sperm production, breast and prostate enlargement, decreased hormone levels, and sterility;

- Sexual and reproductive disorders in females: menstrual irregularities; infertility; masculinizing effects such as facial hair, diminished breast size, and permanently deepened voice;

- Mood swings (including manic-like symptoms leading to violence);

- Impaired judgment (stemming from feelings of invincibility);

- Depression, nervousness, or extreme irritability;

- Delusions; and

- Hostility and aggression.[33]

Human growth hormone also poses risks when used in large doses by athletes. Dr. Alan Rogol testified before a Congressional committee:

It should be noted that off-label use comes with increased risk. One risk factor is that most off-label users are usually unaware of the correct doses (at least for athletes) and one can only assume that the doses administered to athletes must be much greater than those used for the legitimate uses. . . . As I'm sure you are aware, increased dosages often mean increased risk(s).

With increased doses one might get into the range of acromegaly—a serious disease that results from too much growth hormone in the body. In a child with growth potential this might cause gigantism, but I am unaware of anyone being able to take these doses (and pay for them) in the athletic sphere. It should be noted that acromegaly is a serious disease with weak muscle and very significant heart disease.[33]

(Acromegaly is the disease that caused professional wrestler and actor "Andre the Giant" to grow to 7 feet, 4 inches tall (2.24 meters) and 500 pounds (227 kilograms) and ultimately caused his heart to fail.)

Sports leagues are violating the trust of paying fans and taxpayers.

The sports business has changed dramatically in the last few decades. Up until relatively recently, professional sports were an entertainment option available to families who could afford to go to the ballpark or arena for an afternoon or evening of fun, without worrying too much about the cost. Professional athletes lived in the same neighborhoods as average fans, and communities felt an affinity with athletes, who tended to stay with one or two teams for longer periods of time than athletes do today.

As superstar athletes began commanding staggering contracts, owners sought ways to pay multimillion-dollar salaries and continue to make money. Owners built new ballparks with luxury suites that could be rented to businesses. Team owners also sought public financial support for new stadiums and arenas, often threatening to move the team to another city or outside the city limits in order to get the local government to commit millions—often hundreds of millions—in funding for teams' new homes.

Some athletes, even those who have denied using steroids personally, blame the prevalence of steroids on a desire to give fans an exciting product. The problem with that theory is that public investment in sports teams creates a duty to behave in a manner befitting the trust that the public has put into the teams. As Congressman Tim Murphy of Pennsylvania said during a congressional hearing:

> I am concerned that we see comments coming out that can best be described as callous, self-centered, and greedy . . . pervades sports and athletes, when they make comments such as saying it is entertainment, and the fans are expecting us to get out there and have some hits and score touchdowns, and to make goals.[34]

As public figures, athletes should agree to tests that determine whether they are competing fairly.

In the professional sports leagues, with testing procedures governed by labor laws, players' unions have raised privacy concerns in pushing back against proposed testing programs. The major U.S. professional leagues have each instituted their own program, and none of them has adopted a program allowing for blood testing or storing of samples for later testing, as is done in professional cycling and international competition.

Although athletes' privacy is important, opposing drug testing on the grounds of privacy puts athletes at risk. Many individual athletes have spoken in favor of stronger testing measures because testing procedures that enable some athletes to continue doping puts those athletes at risk and puts pressure on other athletes to use performance-enhancing drugs themselves.

Jerry Colangelo, an owner of NBA and MLB teams, took issue with the MLB Players Association's opposition to random drug testing on the grounds of privacy. He told a Congressional committee that baseball players' privacy could be respected, and that the NFL's and NBA's testing programs protected both players' privacy and their health:

> In the NBA, as it is in the NFL, privacy, which seems to be the big obstacle, you know, as far as the [MLB] Players Association is concerned, can be dealt with, again, because there is a partnership that exists: one, to educate the players; number two, to help those who have a problem, and they have the opportunity to come forward and be helped. But, you know, if people make mistakes over and over again, then you have to deal with it. It's a privilege to be a professional athlete. It is not an entitlement, and rules are rules.[35]

Additionally, professional athletes lead very public lives and already give up a lot of their privacy in order to sign huge contracts. And there are other instances of screenings and examinations that are not prompted by drug use allegations. For example, when negotiating a trade to another team, players undergo comprehensive physical examinations. It is therefore difficult to explain why a simple blood test would be so intrusive, when players are subject to other medical tests at other times. Under WADA drug-testing standards, testers take about 0.1 ounce (3 milliliters) of blood, which is comparable to or less than what would be taken in a routine physical.

Being in the public eye, players are subject to gossip, including gossip about steroids. Many people believe that the public has a right to know if children's heroes are taking illegal substances. Donald Hooton, whose teenage son committed suicide after following a steroid regimen, blasted ballplayers at a Congressional hearing: "Your union leaders . . . want us to be sensitive to your right of privacy. Rights of privacy? What about our rights as parents, our rights to expect that the adults our kids all look up to will be held to a standard that does not include behavior that is dangerous, felonious, and . . . cheating."[36]

Summary

The use of performance-enhancing drugs continues to pervade sports at many levels of competition. In international competition and some sports such as professional cycling, extremely strict testing procedures exist, yet athletes continue to try to beat the system through methods such as using newly developed drugs or timing their drug use so as to avoid detection. Nevertheless, many continue to be caught.

In the major sports leagues in the United States, by contrast, testing procedures remain lax by international standards. The labor unions representing the players have fought against stricter testing, putting their own members at great risk by allowing them to continue to ingest harmful substances. Furthermore, the failure to address the issue of performance-enhancing drugs is a breach of public trust. Taxpayers who fund stadiums and fans who buy tickets and merchandise deserve to see a fair competition, not a contest fueled by illegal and dangerous drugs.

Congressional Action on Performance-enhancing Drug Use Is Improper

One of the principle powers of Congress is the duty to regulate interstate commerce—business that takes place among enterprises in different states. Although this category certainly includes professional sports leagues made up of teams that travel the country and have national television deals, Congress has not always been so eager to regulate them.

Outfielder Curt Flood found out the hard way about Congress's reluctance to regulate baseball. After a number of successful years with the St. Louis Cardinals, in which he won seven Golden Glove awards and also enjoyed some success at the plate, Flood suddenly was informed by telephone one day that he had been traded to the Philadelphia Phillies. At the time, player contracts included a "reserve clause," which essentially meant that they could be bound to a single team for their entire careers and could be traded at any time.

Rather than accept the trade to the Phillies, Flood wrote to baseball commissioner Bowie Kuhn and demanded that he make Flood a "free agent," even though free agency did not exist at the time. A free agent is an athlete who is not under contract with a particular team, and because of this can make his or her own professional decisions regarding trades. When Kuhn refused, Flood sued on the grounds that the reserve clause in player contracts violated federal antitrust laws. Antitrust laws are designed to prevent powerful companies from establishing monopolies, stifling competition so that the company can dominate the marketplace and charge whatever price it wants for its goods or services. Yet, for many decades, Major League Baseball has enjoyed just such a monopoly. At one time, various baseball leagues vied for fans' attention, but the joint venture of the American League and the National League has made the prospect for potential competitors very bleak. Without competition from another league, players who wanted to play at the highest level had little choice but to accept the terms offered by MLB clubs.

Flood's case made it all the way to the Supreme Court. He hoped to prevail even though earlier Supreme Court decisions had held that baseball, merely a game, was not considered to be interstate commerce. By the time of Flood's lawsuit, however, baseball had indeed become big business, and he hoped to convince the court that baseball was a form of interstate commerce subject to antitrust laws. The court had already ruled that the NBA and the NFL, as well as other professional sports, were subject to antitrust laws.

Flood succeeded in convincing the court that baseball was indeed interstate commerce, but unfortunately for him, that was not enough to sway the court in his favor. Instead, the court observed that Congress had known for years that Major League Baseball was acting in an anticompetitive manner, and yet had done nothing.

Professional baseball is a business and it is engaged in interstate commerce. . . . With its reserve system enjoying exemption from the federal antitrust laws, baseball is, in a very distinct sense, an exception and an anomaly. . . . [However,] since 1922 baseball, with full and continuing congressional awareness, has been allowed to develop and to expand unhindered by federal legislative action. Remedial legislation has been introduced repeatedly in Congress but none has ever been enacted. The Court, accordingly, has concluded that Congress as yet has had no intention to subject baseball's reserve system to the reach of the antitrust statutes. This, obviously, has been deemed to be something other than mere congressional silence and passivity.[37]

A few years later, an arbitrator struck down the reserve clause. MLB and its players agreed to free agency, which has been modified through collective bargaining between the players' union and the league. Congress, however, has never acted to subject MLB to antitrust laws, giving the league great control over its member clubs. Numerous owners of NHL, NFL, and NBA clubs have relocated their teams (some more than once) since the *Flood* decision, sometimes by threatening to sue the league under antitrust laws for stifling competition for business income. By contrast, only one baseball team has relocated—the financially struggling Montreal Expos, which had been bought out by the league.

Congress has more important concerns than sports.

Although the nation marveled at Mark McGwire and Sammy Sosa's home run contest, the allegations of steroid use that grabbed headlines in the following years threatened to change Congress's hands-off approach toward professional sports. The sports leagues responded internally to performance-enhancing drug use, though, and much of the public thinks that Congress should stay out of the debate. In fact, while Congress was considering legislation in 2005 to mandate drug testing in Major League Baseball, an ABC News/ESPN poll found that

64 percent of Americans felt that MLB should be fully responsible for drug testing, while only 30 percent felt that Congress
should be involved.[38] Americans felt this way about congressional involvement even though they expressed great disapproval
of performance-enhancing drug use: 62 percent of Americans believed that athletes found to have used performance-
enhancing drugs should have their sports records removed
from the books, and 66 percent believed that athletes guilty of
doping should be excluded from the Hall of Fame.[39]

With the nation still mired in an unpopular war in Iraq, the
stock market posting increasing losses day after day, the housing
market sinking, thousands of Americans defaulting on mortgages
they cannot afford, and dozens of other issues to deal with, a congressional committee spent much of February 2008 concentrating
on steroid use in baseball. Roger Clemens and his former trainer
Brian McNamee were called to testify before the committee.
Ostensibly, the purpose of the hearing was to determine whether
the Mitchell Report was an accurate portrayal of the steroid problem in baseball, but ultimately it was a "he said-he said" to determine whether Clemens or McNamee was telling the truth.

Like much of what goes on in politics, the hearing was split
along party lines, with Republican lawmakers generally ham-
mering McNamee about his past lies, in which he covered up
alleged steroid and HGH use by Clemens and fellow major
leaguers Andy Pettitte and Chuck Knoblauch. Although Pettitte
and Knoblauch admitted McNamee injected them with banned
substances, Clemens angrily denied it—although, in a stunning
revelation, Clemens admitted that McNamee had supplied Clemens's wife with HGH with the pitcher's knowledge. Incredu-
lous Democrats tended to question why the committee should
examine the veracity of McNamee's admissions of wrongdoing
involving Roger Clemens when his admissions involving Debbie
Clemens, Pettitte, and Knoblauch had been corroborated.

On the day that several cable networks, including CNN,
carried the Clemens hearings live, CNN's Jack Cafferty reacted

angrily to Congress's decision to hold the hearings. On his blog, he wrote: "Let's see, we have the subprime [mortgage] mess, the housing crisis, a possible recession, the war in Iraq, health care, Social Security, terrorism, and this is what takes up our time—worrying about whether Roger Clemens used steroids a decade ago?"[40]

Many criticized some members of Congress, saying that the legislators acted more like adoring schoolchildren meeting baseball heroes than elected officials who were conducting an investigation. *Sports Illustrated* baseball writer Tom Verducci wrote: "Did you catch Virginia Foxx (R-N.C.) at the conclusion of the hearing? One minute she's asking [Clemens] questions, the next she's holding the arm of Clemens and then giving Debbie Clemens a hug. Ugh."[41]

Athletes have a right to privacy.

Some members of Congress have stated that the public has a right to know whether professional athletes are using performance-enhancing drugs. However, the basis for that right is not clear. The public certainly has a right to know whether airline pilots or school bus drivers are using illegal drugs, but that is a matter of safety. Oddly, Congress is proposing that the federal government require testing professional athletes for drugs more frequently than the government requires testing of airline pilots for illegal drug use. The Federal Aviation Administration (FAA) sets standards for the drug testing of airline pilots, and currently requires that airlines randomly test 25 percent of employees in safety-sensitive positions (such as pilots) for illegal drugs, and 10 percent of employees in safety-sensitive positions for alcohol use on the job.[42]

One of the primary arguments in favor of steroid testing is that professional athletes are role models for young people, but not all athletes are comfortable with that role. Basketball legend Charles Barkley, throughout his career, tried to separate what he did on the court and what he did in his personal life. He infamously declared, "I am not a role model," pointing out that very few young people would ever have a shot at playing professional basketball, and that many people who were good at playing basketball ended up in prison. Although he was widely criticized for his remarks, he stood by them and even starred in a television commercial for Nike in which he (ironically, perhaps) repeated his famous line.

In a collection of essays on sports ethics, author Christopher Wellman imagines a fictional dialogue between Barkley and fellow basketball legend Karl Malone. In it, Wellman describes the outspoken Barkley bristling at the idea that athletes can be held responsible for young people: "Parents are principally responsible for their children taking me as a moral role model in the first place (since a well-nurtured child would not view me as a paragon of virtue merely because of the things I can do on a basketball court)."[43]

Although professional athletes might be public figures, they are still entitled to a private life. The type of drug testing called for by WADA and endorsed by some members of Congress, however, is very intrusive. Floyd Landis, whose contested doping test results led to his suspension from cycling and forfeit of his Tour de France title, recalls a visit from USADA collectors during the time that he was contesting his test results: "The next morning at 7 A.M. doping control rang the doorbell forcefully. . . . There were two collectors this time. . . . They explained to me that now I was required to take my shirt off in addition to pulling my pants down in front of them. So the three of us went into my bathroom and I got naked and peed in the cup."[44]

Professional sports leagues have already established, through collective bargaining with their players' unions, standards for testing that they believe strike a reasonable balance between player privacy and the integrity of the game.

Collectively bargained drug-testing procedures are preferable to legislative mandates.

When representatives of the four major sports leagues were once again called to appear before Congress in February 2008, their frustration was evident. The Mitchell Report had brought to light widespread steroid use prior to Major League Baseball's establishment of a testing program. Since the time of the report, though, each of the leagues had established a testing program that league officials and union representatives felt was both fair and effective. Nevertheless, officials faced questions by members of Congress who wanted to impose stricter testing requirements or take away control of testing from the leagues and players' unions.

Many have questioned whether the massive bureaucracy of the federal government could handle the difficult task of policing performance-enhancing drug use. As Roger Goodell and Gene Upshaw pointed out in the testimony they submitted to Congress:

> [The NFL's testing policy] allows for a rapid response to changing conditions—it is no accident that our collectively-bargained program banned androstenedione and ephedra long before the federal government, or that we were able to retest every specimen in the laboratory's possession (more than 2,000) when the designer steroid THG was first identified. . . .
>
> When the FDA banned ephedra, the effect of the ban was sharply limited by a federal judge. When the NFL and NFLPA agreed to ban ephedra, it stayed banned.[45]

Sports leagues are also opposed to having testing taken out of their hands and placed into the control of a third party like the USADA. Although the USADA and its parent agency, WADA, are supposed to be impartial, many have criticized the fairness of their procedures. In his book, cyclist Floyd Landis criticized the federal government's support of USADA: "USADA wrote its own rules, it enforces them, it acts as prosecutor in legal cases, and it picks which judges hear each case. . . . Most of USADA's funding comes from Congress, so why is it allowed to have a system of justice in which it is the lawmaker, the police, the prosecution, and the jury?"[46]

Jose Canseco has charged that MLB and team officials not only knew about widespread steroid use in baseball, but that they also actively encouraged it. Above, Canseco signs a copy of his book *Juiced*, in which he credits much of his success to his use of steroids and claims that he suffered no ill health effects.

NBA commissioner David Stern echoed Landis's sentiments, noting that the NBA and its players' union, like other professional sports leagues, had set up testing programs that were independent of the league but operated according to principles of fairness established in the collective bargaining process. Stern testified to Congress:

> We do not believe that the involvement of an entity like WADA will improve our Program in any respect. . . . The NBA's Program is already managed by independent entities and individuals with substantial expertise and integrity. Moreover, because the NBA and the Players Association jointly created our Program, NBA players have confidence in its legitimacy and impartiality, and that trust is critical to making the Program run smoothly.[47]

Mandatory drug testing of athletes raises constitutional concerns.

Whether or not it is sound public policy to require drug testing in professional sports leagues, any law passed by Congress must comply with the U.S. Constitution. Critics of mandatory drug-testing laws suggest that these laws might violate one or more provisions of the Constitution and therefore could not be enforced by the federal government.

Critics suggest that mandatory drug testing amounts to an illegal search and seizure in violation of the Fourth Amendment to the Constitution. The Fourth Amendment protects the populace from invasive police tactics. Prior to the establishment of the United States, English authorities used a "general warrant" that allowed them to gather evidence of crimes by searching people and places without any reason for suspicion. As a result, nobody could feel secure from intrusion.

The writers of the Constitution believed that the authorities should only search for evidence of crime or seize property if they had a sound basis for doing so. The Fourth Amendment states:

"The right of the people to be secure in their persons, houses, papers, and effects, against unreasonable searches and seizures, shall not be violated, and no Warrants shall issue, but upon probable cause, supported by Oath or affirmation, and particularly describing the place to be searched, and the persons or things to be seized."[48] In general, therefore, the government cannot gather evidence unless it has a specific reason to suspect someone of wrongdoing. It cannot randomly search for evidence, as would be the case with random drug tests of the general population. For this reason, a law that, for example, allowed police to go door-to-door demanding urine samples would be invalid.

Although the text of the Fourth Amendment seems plain and clear, the U.S. Supreme Court, in its interpretation of the amendment, has carved out a number of exceptions to the general rule requiring individual suspicion for searches and seizures. One such exception is the so-called "special needs" doctrine (general legal principle). This doctrine applies to administrative searches, or ones in which the evidence is not being gathered for the purposes of a criminal prosecution. According to the doctrine, as Justice Anthony Kennedy explained in the 1989 case *Skinner v. Railway Labor Executives' Association*: "In limited circumstances, where the privacy interests implicated by the search are minimal, and where an important governmental interest furthered by the intrusion would be placed in jeopardy by a requirement of individualized suspicion, a search may be reasonable despite the absence of such suspicion."[49]

At issue in the *Skinner* case was a Federal Railroad Administration (FRA) regulation requiring railroads to test employees for drugs and alcohol if they had been involved in a crash, and authorizing railroads to test employees who violated certain safety rules. The court upheld the regulation. Although the drug tests at issue were not random—because the employees were involved in accidents or had violated safety rules—the tests did not require any sort of suspicion that the employee had used alcohol or drugs. The Supreme Court held:

The Government interest in testing without a showing of individualized suspicion is compelling. Employees subject to the tests discharge duties fraught with such risks of injury to others that even a momentary lapse of attention can have disastrous consequences. Much like persons who have routine access to dangerous nuclear power facilities ... employees who are subject to testing under the FRA regulations can cause great human loss before any signs of impairment become noticeable to supervisors or others. An impaired employee, the FRA found, will seldom display any outward "signs detectable by the lay person or, in many cases, even the physician."[50]

Similarly, in *Treasury Employees v. Von Raab*, the Supreme Court upheld drug testing of U.S. Customs and Border Protection agents involved in international drug law enforcement. The justices noted the special need for officers involved in drug law enforcement to be free from the temptations of the drug dealer whom they were required to intercept:

Many of the Service's employees are often exposed to [the international] criminal element and to the controlled substances it seeks to smuggle into the country. . . . It is readily apparent that the Government has a compelling interest in ensuring that front-line interdiction personnel are physically fit, and have unimpeachable integrity and judgment.[51]

A common link between the *Skinner* and *Von Raab* cases is that both cases involved drug testing of people involved in an activity (operating trains and intercepting drug smugglers) that is highly controlled by the federal government and directly linked to public safety. If a train engineer or a customs agent were to be impaired by drug use, other people could be placed at risk.

But the Supreme Court took the logic of *Skinner* and *Von Raab* a step further in a 1995 case, *Vernonia School District v.*

Acton, allowing the random drug testing of high school athletes. A local school district had instituted testing for recreational drugs such as cocaine and marijuana in response to concerns that high school athletes were at the center of the school district's drug culture. The court found that the school procedures—which required an observer to watch male athletes from behind while the athletes stood at a urinal, and to listen to female athletes collect a urine sample in a closed toilet stall—did not amount to a significant invasion of privacy:

> These conditions are nearly identical to those typically encountered in public restrooms, which men, women, and especially school children use daily. Under such conditions, the privacy interests compromised by the process of obtaining the urine sample are in our view negligible. The other privacy-invasive aspect of urinalysis is, of course, the information it discloses concerning the state of the subject's body, and the materials he has ingested. In this regard it is significant that the tests at issue here look only for drugs, and not for whether the student is, for example, epileptic, pregnant, or diabetic.[52]

It might seem that the court's ruling in this line of cases would support random drug testing of professional athletes. Opponents of drug testing, however, distinguish the testing of professional athletes from the testing of U.S. Customs agents or high school athletes. Critics would instead try to persuade the courts to rely on the logic of another Supreme Court decision that struck down a Georgia law requiring candidates for public office to submit to random drug testing.

In *Chandler v. Miller*, the court distinguished drug testing for political candidates, noting that adults have greater expectations of privacy from government intrusion than children have from their schools. The court noted: "The program's context was critical [in *Vernonia*], for local governments bear large 'responsibilities, under a public school system, as guardian and tutor of children entrusted to its care.' . . . Our decision noted that 'students within the school environment have a lesser expectation of privacy than members of the population generally.' "[53]

Opponents of drug testing could argue that the situation of professional athletes playing sports almost entirely unregulated by the federal government is a far cry from the situation of high school athletes, whose parents have entrusted them to the school. In fact, an attorney for the Congressional Research Service, conducting background research for lawmakers attempting to enact steroid legislation, acknowledged that the unique relationship between the state government–run schools and student athletes appears to cancel out any value of precedent that the *Vernonia School District* case might have.[54]

Another potential argument for opponents of testing is that Congress is trying to compromise the privacy of professional athletes not to protect the athletes themselves, but instead to prevent professional athletes from glorifying the use of performance-enhancing drugs. The *Chandler* court pointed out that the earlier *Von Raab* decision had rejected the idea that an individual's rights could be taken away in order to send a message about an organization's integrity:

> In *Von Raab*, the Customs Service had defended its officer drug test program in part as a way to demonstrate the agency's commitment to enforcement of the law. . . . The *Von Raab* Court, however, did not rely on that justification. Indeed . . . a need of the "set a good example" genre [is not] sufficient to overwhelm a Fourth Amendment objection. . . .[55]

The *Chandler* court cited an earlier dissent by Justice Louis Brandeis, who had warned in 1928 that well-meaning laws could threaten individual freedom:

> Experience should teach us to be most on our guard to protect liberty when the Government's purposes are beneficent. Men born to freedom are naturally alert to repel invasion of

their liberty by evil-minded rulers. The greatest dangers to liberty lurk in insidious encroachment by men of zeal, well meaning but without understanding.[56]

Heeding the admonition of Justice Brandeis, the *Chandler* court refused to allow Georgia to tread on the privacy rights of individuals running for office, without any reason for suspecting their drug use, simply to ensure that public officials "set a good example" for the state's citizens. In striking down the law,

Justice O'Connor's dissent in *Vernonia School District v. Acton*

When the majority of the U.S. Supreme Court upheld random drug testing of high school athletes, Justice Sandra Day O'Connor, joined by two other justices, dissented on the grounds that randomly testing students for drug use, rather than testing only those suspected of drug use, was a violation of the basic principles of the Fourth Amendment:

The Court dispenses with a requirement of individualized suspicion on considered policy grounds. First, it explains that precisely because every student athlete is being tested, there is no concern that school officials might act arbitrarily in choosing who to test. Second, a broad-based search regime, the Court reasons, dilutes the accusatory nature of the search. In making these policy arguments, of course, the Court sidesteps powerful, countervailing privacy concerns. Blanket searches, because they can involve "thousands or millions" of searches, "pos[e] a greater threat to liberty" than do suspicion-based ones, which "affec[t] one person at a time." ... Searches based on individualized suspicion also afford potential targets considerable control over whether they will, in fact, be searched because a person can avoid such a search by not acting in an objectively suspicious way. And given that the surest way to avoid acting suspiciously is to avoid the underlying wrongdoing, the costs of such a regime, one would think, are minimal.

the court noted: "However well meant, the candidate drug test Georgia has devised diminishes personal privacy for a symbol's sake. The Fourth Amendment shields society against that state action."[57]

Testifying to Congress, MLB's Players Association head Donald Fehr noted:

> Any legislation governing drug testing in private industry surely raises troubling constitutional questions. . . . [The

> But whether a blanket search is "better"...than a regime based on individualized suspicion is not a debate in which we should engage. In my view, it is not open to judges or government officials to decide on policy grounds which is better and which is worse. For most of our constitutional history, mass, suspicionless searches have been generally considered per se unreasonable within the meaning of the Fourth Amendment. And we have allowed exceptions in recent years only where it has been clear that a suspicion-based regime would be ineffectual. Because that is not the case here, I dissent.

O'Connor did agree that random drug testing might be a convenient and effective way of catching drug users, although the Fourth Amendment guarantees that individuals will not be subjected to being "rounded up" for no particular reason:

> It remains the law that the police cannot, say, subject to drug testing every person entering or leaving a certain drug-ridden neighborhood in order to find evidence of crime.... And this is true even though it is hard to think of a more compelling government interest than the need to fight the scourge of drugs on our streets and in our neighborhoods. Nor could it be otherwise, for if being evenhanded were enough to justify evaluating a search regime under an open-ended balancing test, the Warrant Clause, which presupposes that there is some category of searches for which individualized suspicion is non-negotiable ... would be a dead letter.

Source: *Vernonia School Dist. 47J v. Acton*, 515 U.S. 646 (1995) (O'Connor, J., dissenting).

Chandler] Court determined that the stated intention of having candidates set a good example was not sufficient to justify
the inherent invasion of privacy. It is likely that a law governing drug testing in professional sports would face a serious
challenge as well.[58]

A further distinction that opponents of mandated drug testing can make is that, unlike the subjects of testing in *Von Raab*,
Skinner, and *Vernonia*, professional athletes are already subject
to drug testing. Unlike proposals by Congress to legally mandate
drug testing, the current system (in which leagues and players'
unions collectively agree to drug-testing policies) does not present constitutional concerns because no governmental action
is involved. The Fourth Amendment applies only to local, state,
and federal governments, not to private entities such as sports
teams or leagues. Thus, to uphold the law, the government would
need to demonstrate that its interest in testing athletes above
and beyond the current testing regimen is compelling enough to
overcome the invasion of athletes' privacy.

Summary

In recent years, Congress has repeatedly held hearings on the use
of performance-enhancing drugs in professional sports, with
individual members of Congress introducing various proposals
to require testing of professional athletes. Although the professional sports leagues were initially hesitant to institute or step up
testing, all of the leagues now have random testing policies and
mandatory suspensions for users of performance-enhancing
drugs.

Critics of congressional action in this arena argue that Congress has more important concerns than requiring drug testing
of athletes who are already subjected to more rigorous drug testing than are people upon whom the public's safety depends, such
as pilots. Critics dismiss broad arguments that the public has a
"right to know" about athletes' drug use, noting that the leagues

have collectively bargained with their players' unions to establish testing procedures that ensure both detection of drug use and respect for players' privacy and right to challenge positive tests. Some have also questioned whether congressional action would even withstand constitutional challenges, given that the U.S. Supreme Court has invalidated a law requiring drug testing of political candidates.

Congressional Intervention Is Needed to Restore Public Confidence in Professional Sports

For several years, members of Congress have tried unsuccessfully to pass legislation addressing the use of illegal performance-enhancing drugs in professional sports. The federal government has used existing laws to pursue those who supply performance-enhancing drugs to athletes, as it did in the prosecution of BALCO's Victor Conte. As a secondary tactic, the government has sought to prosecute high-profile athletes such as Barry Bonds, Marion Jones, and Roger Clemens for perjury (allegedly lying under oath about performance-enhancing drug use).

But the federal government has failed to act in any systematic way against what the public perceives to be widespread use of performance-enhancing drugs in professional sports. This is in part because professional sports leagues have been relatively uncooperative in Congress's efforts. On March 17, 2005, many

Barry Bonds hit his seventy-third home run of the season in October 2001, shown in progress in this photo. In an attempt to quell the increasing use of performance-enhancing drugs, the U.S. government has prosecuted high-profile athletes like Bonds.

eyes were focused on Capitol Hill when Congress called for questioning Mark McGwire and Sammy Sosa—whose home run duel had electrified the nation—as well as outspoken steroid-user Jose Canseco and fellow ballplayers Rafael Palmeiro, Curt Schilling, and Frank Thomas.

If Americans were hoping to get any insight into steroid use in baseball, they, like Congress, were sorely disappointed. Sosa, who in the past had always been willing to give interviews in English to the media, showed up with an interpreter and at times seemed to have lost his ability to speak English. An exasperated Congressman Dennis Kucinich even asked him a question in Spanish. During the same proceedings, McGwire infamously declared, "I'm not here to talk about the past, I'm here to talk about the positive and not the negative about this issue,"[59] steadfastly refusing to answer questions as to whether he had ever used steroids. Palmeiro, emphatically pointing his finger, declared, "I have never used steroids, period. I do not know how to say it any more clearly than that."[60] Major League Baseball later suspended Palmeiro after he tested positive for steroids.

The sight of the game's heroes giving vague and evasive answers did not help to improve baseball's image. Unfortunately, the congressional investigation also did not give Congress much to work with in drafting legislation. Former Senator George Mitchell conducted an investigation of performance-enhancing drug use, however, and released a comprehensive report in late 2007. With that, Congress once again revisited the issue of combating performance-enhancing drug use in MLB as well as in the NFL, the NHL, and the NBA.

Eliminating controlled substance use from professional athletics is a legitimate government concern.

Many have criticized Congress for holding hearings about drug use in professional sports when seemingly so many other issues face the nation. Senator Jim Bunning, once an elite athlete himself, defended the importance of Congress's investigation of baseball:

> Some in the press have talked about this hearing like it's a lark. It isn't. Congress is dead serious. We have every right to be concerned that the national pastime and all that it represents has been threatened by the selfish actions of a few.
>
> Baseball is . . . a multibillion-dollar business that affects our economy and most of our largest communities. There's no doubt that Congress has a direct and important interest in what happens in baseball.[61]

Charged with the task of investigating the constitutionality of proposed congressional legislation, an attorney for the Congressional Research Service (CRS) identified some potential "compelling interests" that would justify mandatory testing for performance-enhancing drugs.

One possible justification identified in the CRS report is that performance-enhancing drugs pose a risk not only to the user, but also to those who compete against athletes using the drugs. Drugs pose a risk to others involved in the game, too, such as coaches and referees on the field. The report speculated, "Medical evidence could be mustered in the course of ongoing congressional hearings of the adverse health effects, not only to the steroid users, but to the safety of other players."[62] Although such an argument might seem far-fetched, many attribute high rates of injury in certain sports to the strength and speed of today's athletes—physical characteristics that can be bolstered by the use of steroids and other performance-enhancing drugs. Consider the following examples:

- In baseball, batted balls can be deadly. In July 2007, Mike Coolbaugh, the first-base coach for the minor league Tulsa Drillers, was killed at age 35 by a line drive as he stood near the base.

- The NFL has ongoing problems with concussions. Despite improvements in helmet designs, players are being hit hard and hurt by bigger, faster opponents. Some studies suggest that NFL players are at a greater risk of depression, Alzheimer's disease, and loss of mental function later in life as a result of head trauma sustained while playing football.

- The size and speed of NHL players has increased dramatically, and though helmets became mandatory in the 1990s, the rate of concussions has actually increased. Players, league officials, and outside observers disagree about the reason for the NHL's concussion problem, with some attributing it to the increased size and speed of the players, others linking it to players showing less restraint now that everyone is helmeted, and others saying that a higher percentage of concussions are simply being reported now (and that concussions are not necessarily increasing).

The other potentially compelling interest in controlling steroid use among professional athletes, according to the CRS report, is that "protecting the integrity of the game may be particularly important given the demonstrable influence of professional athletes on young players at all levels."[63]

Congress seems to have placed the motivation to prevent steroid use among youth as its primary reason for addressing the problem at the professional level. Texan Donald Hooton appeared before Congress, describing how his son committed suicide after starting to use steroids when his coach told him he needed to get bigger and stronger. After his son's suicide, many young athletes told Hooton that they, too, had felt pressured to use steroids in order to succeed. In addition to peer pressure and the drive to succeed, Hooton blamed the influence of professional athletes:

Many factors contribute to the high usage of steroids amongst our kids, including the pressure to win and earn a scholarship, combined with heavy peer pressure. I believe a major contributor is the example, the poor example being set by our professional teams, athletes, and management. Our kids look up to these guys. They want to do the things that the pros do to be successful.[64]

He derisively addressed the claims made by some athletes that they unknowingly used performance-enhancing drugs (particularly Barry Bonds, who claimed that he thought he was using flaxseed oil and arthritic balm rather than steroids):

Let me take this opportunity to speak directly to players like Barry Bonds and others, who insult our intelligence by claiming that they do not know what they have been taking to improve their performance. Barry, gentlemen, the next time you are wondering what the stuff is that is causing you to gain the muscle and strength that allows you to hit so many home runs, just ask any high school baseball player in America. They know exactly what you have been taking to get those results, and they are following your lead. Our youngsters hear the message. It is loud, it is clear, and it is wrong: If you want to achieve your goals, it is okay to use steroids, because the pros are doing it.[65]

Steroid use among high school students has declined in the years since the professional leagues have implemented or strengthened testing policies, perhaps suggesting that tackling the problem at the professional level has had a trickle-down effect. According to the National Institute on Drug Abuse, lifetime steroid use among twelfth graders has declined from 3.4 percent in 2004 to 2.2 percent in 2007. Past-year use has declined from 2.5 percent to 1.4 percent.[66] These are percentages of the entire student body, however—not just athletes. Many people remain concerned about the influence that professional athletes have on the nation's youth.

Professional athletes are public figures who should be held to high standards.

In addition to the matter of influencing drug use by young people, some would say that having sports leagues in which illegal drug use is rampant is an affront to society. In one hearing on baseball, North Dakota Senator Byron Dorgan said:

> So let me just say, as a fan of this wonderful sport, that I want this sport to produce splendid athletes [who] can be role models for America's youngsters. But I certainly don't want to see America's pastime become a pastime in which these wonderful athletes engage in the use of performance-enhancing drugs in order to make it. That is not what baseball should be about. Drugs have no place in our culture, and certainly not in America's big-league ballparks.[67]

Kentucky Senator Jim Bunning talked about baseball as a national treasure that was being ruined by the misdeeds of current players:

> The players and Major League Baseball must be held accountable for the integrity of the game. After all, it's not their game. It's ours; they're just enjoying the privilege of playing it for a short time. What I may think many of today's players don't understand is that many others came before them and even more will come after them. And all of us have an obligation to protect the integrity of the greatest game ever invented. Now the game of baseball has been tarnished by some players because they didn't follow the rules and thought they were bigger than the game. It is disturbing to see trends continuing today. Baseball has to follow the rules just like everyone else. If a player thinks they are above the law of the land and can

defy a congressional subpoena, they are sadly mistaken. They are not bigger than the game and they are certainly not bigger than the law of the land.[68]

Bunning also criticized owners, going so far as to suggest that they built new ballparks (often with taxpayer support) that encouraged players to take steroids for the purpose of hitting home runs: "The same goes for owners. For over a decade, they have turned their heads when it came to steroids. They have helped put the game at risk. Not only did they turn a blind eye, they built smaller parks, making it easier to hit home runs. The balls started flying farther. We have to ask why all of these things happened."[69]

Sports leagues cannot be trusted to police themselves.

In February 2008, Congressman Bobby Rush's subcommittee called the heads of the four major sports leagues to testify. He expressed his belief that the leagues' testing procedures were still not adequate: "In spite of the fact that they want to pronounce that they have it under control, I still think that it's not fully under control, and we have to do more."[70]

The same subcommittee had held similar hearings a few years earlier, but no legislation passed. Congressman Joe Barton said, "Let's get it right this time. . . . Let's go ahead and get something into law that is acceptable. It's no fun having this hearing every two to three years."[71]

Jose Canseco has charged that MLB officials and team officials not only knew about widespread steroid use, but that they also actively encouraged it. Baseball had been struggling since the 1994 strike that led to the cancellation of the World Series that year. Then Sammy Sosa and Mark McGwire began their dual assault upon Roger Maris's single-season home run record. With renewed fan interest, Canseco alleges, team owners encouraged the use of performance-enhancing drugs by

Professional Sports Responsibility Act of 2005

Congress has introduced, but not yet passed, a number of bills to mandate testing of professional athletes for performance-enhancing drugs. This bill from the House of Representatives is one example of an unsuccessful bill.

SEC. 2. FINDINGS.

Congress finds the following:

(1) Congress has created some important legal benefits for professional sports leagues, some of which have been instrumental to the enormous success of those leagues. These benefits include antitrust exemptions created under the National Sports Broadcasting Act, labor exemptions to the antitrust laws to engage in collective bargaining agreements, special visas for foreign professional athletes, and several tax benefits including tax write-offs after the sale of a team and tax exemption status for professional sports leagues. Additionally, they enjoy indirect tax benefits which create incentives for cities to build stadiums.

(2) The leagues have no entitlement to these benefits and Congress can revoke these benefits ... at any time. ...

(6) The tolerance of the use of performance-enhancing substances by professional athletes by the professional sports leagues send the wrong message to youth that these drugs must be used to advance in athletic competition.

(7) To continue to enjoy the benefits afforded the leagues by Congress, the leagues must operate as responsible citizens of the United States by adopting strong policies to eliminate the use of these substances and reassure the public that there will be no place in professional sports for the illegal use of performance-enhancing substances or other controlled substances.

(8) As of the date of enactment of this Act, Congress is not satisfied that the four major professional leagues have an appropriate testing and penalty policy in place. Minimum standards for testing for the illegal use of performance-enhancing substances and other controlled substances, and minimum penalties for the illegal use of these substances, should be established.

SEC. 4. STANDARDS FOR TESTING FOR PERFORMANCE-ENHANCING AND OTHER CONTROLLED SUBSTANCES.

   (a) In General: Not later than 180 days after the date of the enactment of this Act, the Attorney General shall issue rules requiring the testing by major professional leagues for the illegal use of steroids and other performance-enhancing substances and any substance designated as a Schedule I substance under the Controlled Substances Act (21 U.S.C. 801 et seq.). The requirements of section 553 of title 5, United States Code, shall not apply to such rulemaking. Such rules shall be issued with regard to each specific major professional league and at a minimum establish—

   (1) the minimum number of times each professional athlete should be tested for prohibited substances during a calendar year, ensuring that tests are conducted at random intervals throughout the season of play and during the off-season;

   (2) the applicable prohibited substances for which professional athletes shall be tested;

   (3) a method of testing and analysis which guarantees that—

      (A) the tests will be administered by an independent party who is not an employee of a major professional league, member team, or labor organization representing professional athletes in that league; and

      (B) the determination of the persons to be tested, and the timing and frequency of testing, is not controlled by the major professional league;

   (4) a means for exempting particular substances that have legitimate medical or therapeutic use, if such use is for a documented medical condition of the professional athlete;

   (5) sufficient penalties for any professional athlete who tests positive for a prohibited substance and penalties for any professional athlete who refuses or fails to submit to a required test;

   (6) an adequate appeals process; and

   (7) procedures for publicly disclosing the identity of any athlete who tests positive for a prohibited substance.

Source: Professional Sports Responsibility Act of 2005, H.R. 3942, 109th Congress, 1st Session (2005).

financially rewarding players who were hitting the ball out of the park: "If the athlete did his part, jabbed himself in the butt with the steroid needle, and grew stronger and tougher and better, the owners did their part and wrote out the checks—which just kept getting bigger all the time."[72] In Canseco's opinion, the owners did this knowingly: "The leadership of baseball made a tacit decision not only to tolerate steroid use, but actually to pretend it didn't exist. . . ."[73]

Although professional sports leagues claim to have created independent testing agencies, anti-doping advocates have questioned the independence of the testing programs. Travis Tygart, chief executive officer of USADA, seemed to imply that testing programs that operated for a single sport, rather than one body serving multiple sports (as USADA did), could not be truly independent: "It is important that 'independence' not be dismissed as simply window dressing designed to remove perceived conflicts. Instead, USADA's experience has established that true independence is a functional and fundamental requirement of an effective anti-doping program."[74]

Part of the problem, Tygart suggested, is that leagues can decide for themselves what constitutes doping: "In fact, true independence is the single most important element of the USADA model because it provides us with complete authority over all areas of the entire anti-doping program."[75] The leagues and the players' unions have an obvious financial interest in maintaining the good reputation of the league—especially its star players—while independent bodies such as USADA have no incentive to protect cheaters:

> Simply put, USADA's mission is to protect clean sport and preserve the rights of athletes to compete clean. In accomplishing that mission, USADA does not have a conflicting duty to also protect the image of the sport it serves or of commercial factors such as obligations to sponsors, owners, or other investors. This true independence frees USADA to

take the steps necessary to accomplish its mission without worrying about the possible negative impact on the financial interests or the image of the sport.

Ultimately, by keeping a steadfast focus on the sole goal of clean sport, USADA has improved the image of Olympic sport, but that victory has necessarily come at the price of exposing the dark side of sport along the way.[76]

Commenting on the Mitchell Report, Tygart suggests that baseball has too much invested in protecting the legacies of star players such as Roger Clemens and Barry Bonds:

When the path to redemption requires that individuals once thought to be heroes must be exposed as frauds, it takes a strong resolve to walk that path. Unfortunately, experience establishes that where that resolve may be impacted by a duty to protect the image of the sport or its profits then the mission will be easily compromised. This point is made resoundingly clear in the Mitchell Report.[77]

In statements to Congress, NFL officials have held out their own testing program as a success that could serve as an example to other leagues. However, anti-doping advocates dismiss the effectiveness of the league's program. Unlike international competition, in which first-time offenders face a lengthy ban and repeat offenders face a lifetime ban, the NFL only bans offenders for four games—a quarter of the 16-game season. Critics John McCloskey and Julian Bailes attack the penalties as inadequate: "Despite [the NFL's] financial commitment to the technological war against modern cheaters, it can be argued that the NFL continues to minimize the problem with its weak penalties."[78]

McCloskey and Bailes also criticize the NFL's analysis of test results, which allow for players to test for a ratio of testosterone to epitestosterone (T/E) of up to 10 to 1. Most tests consider a ratio of 6 to 1 as conclusively positive for doping; a normal ratio is 1 to 1. They write: "The NFL (and the IOC and others that use the 6-to-1 ratio) are leaving a large enough window to cast serious doubt as to the actual number of players who are doping."[79]

Mandatory drug testing has been upheld in the context of athletic competition.

Although some have expressed doubts about the constitutionality of a federal law mandating drug testing of professional athletes, laws requiring testing of employees for drug use have been upheld in many contexts, including athletic competition. In two notable cases, courts have found that random drug testing of athletes was acceptable under the "special needs" doctrine, which requires balancing an important government need against individuals' privacy rights.

In *Vernonia School District v. Acton*, for example, the U.S. Supreme Court upheld random testing of high school athletes for recreational drugs. The Court observed that the school system had a strong need to reduce drug use among students:

> School years are the time when the physical, psychological, and addictive effects of drugs are most severe. . . . And of course the effects of a drug-infested school are visited not just upon the users, but upon the entire student body and faculty, as the educational process is disrupted. In the present case, moreover, the necessity for the State to act is magnified by the fact that this evil is being visited not just upon individuals at large, but upon children for whom it has undertaken a special responsibility of care and direction.[80]

The Court also noted that drug use by athletes created particular risks:

> This program is directed more narrowly to drug use by school athletes, where the risk of immediate physical harm to the drug user or those with whom he is playing his sport is

particularly high. Apart from psychological effects, which include impairment of judgment, slow reaction time, and a lessening of the perception of pain, the particular drugs screened by the District's Policy have been demonstrated to pose substantial physical risks to athletes.[81]

Furthermore, the Court noted that courts had placed limits on the privacy rights of public school students, and that high school athletes had further diminished expectations of privacy because they dressed and showered in communal locker rooms and were subjected to health screenings:

> Legitimate privacy expectations are even less with regard to student athletes. School sports are not for the bashful. They require "suiting up" before each practice or event, and showering and changing afterwards. Public school locker rooms, the usual sites for these activities, are not notable for the privacy they afford. The locker rooms in Vernonia are typical: no individual dressing rooms are provided; shower heads are lined up along a wall, unseparated by any sort of partition or curtain; not even all the toilet stalls have doors. As the United States Court of Appeals for the Seventh Circuit has noted, there is "an element of 'communal undress' inherent in athletic participation."[82]

The Court also found that the student-athletes' privacy rights were diminished because they had voluntarily chosen to participate in athletics:

> There is an additional respect in which school athletes have a reduced expectation of privacy. By choosing to "go out for the team," they voluntarily subject themselves to a degree of regulation even higher than that imposed on students generally. In Vernonia's public schools, they must submit to a preseason physical exam . . . they must acquire adequate insurance

coverage or sign an insurance waiver, maintain a minimum grade point average, and comply with any "rules of conduct, dress, training hours, and related matters as may be established for each sport by the head coach and athletic director with the principal's approval." . . . Somewhat like adults who choose to participate in a "closely regulated industry," students who voluntarily participate in school athletics have reason to expect intrusions upon normal rights and privileges, including privacy.[83]

Another case upheld drug testing of jockeys, but the decision was rendered by a lower court and is not binding throughout the country. In *Shoemaker v. Handel*, the U.S. Court of Appeals for the 3rd Circuit upheld New Jersey's requirement that jockeys involved in state-sanctioned horseracing submit to random drug testing. The court noted that the state racing commission regulated the horseracing industry in many ways, including the licensing of jockeys, trainers, and others. The court observed:

Because the public wagers on the outcome of races, the Commission's regulations have focused upon the necessity for preserving both the fact and the appearance of integrity of the racing performances. Thus, for example, the Commission's regulations for many years have placed on the trainer of a horse the absolute duty, regardless of fault, to protect the horse from the administration of drugs that might affect its performance. . . . Moreover to assure the discharge of this duty, the Commission's regulations have for many years provided for post-race specimen testing of horses and, if tests prove positive for a drug or foreign substance, for warrantless searches of the premises occupied by the stable involved.[84]

Applying the "special needs" doctrine, the court found that the state had a compelling interest in preventing drug abuse by jockeys:

> New Jersey has a strong interest in assuring the public of the
> integrity of the persons engaged in the horseracing industry.
> Public confidence forms the foundation for the success of
> an industry based on wagering. Frequent alcohol and drug
> testing is an effective means of demonstrating that persons
> engaged in the horseracing industry are not subject to cer-
> tain outside influences. It is the public's perception, not the
> known suspicion, that triggers the state's strong interest in
> conducting warrantless testing.[85]

The court also held that jockeys had a reduced privacy interest
because of their involvement in a heavily regulated industry:

> It is also clear that the Commission historically has exercised
> its rulemaking authority in ways that have reduced the justifi-
> able privacy expectations of persons engaged in the horserac-
> ing industry. When jockeys chose to become involved in this
> pervasively regulated business and accepted a state license,
> they did so with the knowledge that the Commission would
> exercise its authority to assure public confidence in the integ-
> rity of the industry. Even before the regulations challenged
> here were adopted, the jockeys were aware that the Commis-
> sion had promulgated regulations providing for warrantless
> searches of stables.[86]

Some of the arguments supporting extending the logic of
Vernonia and *Shoemaker* to professional athletics have already
been discussed. Although professional athletics have many differences from state-regulated horseracing and high school
athletics—one of them being that professional athletics are not as
closely regulated—the public does have a great interest in ensuring that competition is fair. In particular, this includes taxpayers
who subsidize team stadiums and arenas, not to mention those
who bet legally on sports in Nevada. Congress also might have
a legitimate interest in player safety, given the high numbers of

injuries in some sports. Finally, the undeniable influence of professional athletes on the behavior of young people might heighten the government's interest in controlling what goes on in professional sports.

An additional point that could save the constitutionality of mandatory drug testing for professional athletes is that Congress has heard evidence that performance-enhancing drugs are a widespread problem in professional sports. When steroid testing began, it is thought that many athletes shifted to human growth hormone, which is currently undetectable by the urine testing methods to which the players' unions have agreed. Furthermore, some players have chosen undetectable "designer" steroids such as those at the center of the BALCO scandal.

Unlike past cases striking down drug testing, there is significant evidence of need for regulation in professional sports. In the *Chandler* case, which struck down mandatory testing for candidates for political office, the court noted that the court had asked the state's lawyers, "Is there any indication anywhere in this record that Georgia has a particular problem here with State officeholders being drug abusers?"[87] One of the state's lawyers responded, "No, there is no such evidence. . . . and to be frank, there is no such problem as we sit here today."[88] A law requiring mandatory testing of athletes is readily distinguishable from Georgia's law, which the court called "notably lacking in . . . any indication of a concrete danger demanding departure from the Fourth Amendment's main rule."[89]

Summary

Some have questioned whether it is worthwhile for Congress to regulate performance-enhancing drug use in professional sports, while others have questioned whether Congress even has the authority under the Constitution to do so. Supporters of legislation have advanced a number of arguments in favor of legislation, including the widespread nature of the problem, the relative inability of professional sports leagues to police themselves, the need for true independence in testing, the need to protect players' health, and the need to restore public confidence in a multibillion-dollar industry that is based on some of the nation's proudest traditions.

Any legislation passed regarding this issue would be challenged in court, but supporters have a number of legal precedents that can be cited in favor of mandatory testing. Courts have upheld testing of high school athletes and state-licensed jockeys on the basis of protecting athletes and maintaining public confidence. The same could be said of testing for professional athletes. Additionally, unlike testing programs that have been struck down due to lack of need, testing of professional athletes would be based on evidence of a significant problem.

Athletes Need More Freedom to Take Dietary Supplements

Nathan Piasecki, an elite wrestler, was living and working out at the U.S. Olympic Training Center in Colorado. Like many athletes, he frequented health food stores to buy legal dietary supplements. Because some dietary supplements that are legal in the United States are nevertheless banned from Olympic competition, he bought all of his supplements at a local branch of the Vitamin Shoppe, a national chain. It was where many of his fellow athletes purchased their supplements, and where the staff seemed especially knowledgeable.

As a further precaution, Piasecki brought a copy of the USADA's list of prohibited substances with him to the store and advised the sales staff that he could not take anything containing ingredients on the list. As an even further precaution, Piasecki personally compared the ingredients on supplement bottles to the substances on his prohibited list.

In October 2006, the staff at the Vitamin Shoppe recommended a product called 6-OXO as a means of helping Piasecki recover from workouts. The bottle claimed that the product was "naturally occurring," and Piasecki compared the list of ingredients to the prohibited list. Neither 6-OXO nor its active ingredient—4-etioallocholen-3, 6, 17-trione—were on the prohibited list. Before taking the supplement, Piasecki visited the Web site of 6-OXO's manufacturer, Ergopharm, which claimed that the supplement was "naturally occurring, drug-free, [and] legal."[90]

In January 2007, a urine sample provided by Piasecki tested positive for 6-alpha-Hydroandrostenedione, a urine marker that indicates the use of a banned substance. (Because the body breaks down steroids and other performance-enhancing drugs, urine tests typically look for byproducts of banned substances rather than the banned substances themselves.) Initially, Piasecki thought that the supplement had been contaminated with DHEA, a dietary supplement that is legal in the United States but banned from Olympic competition. It was later determined that the active ingredient he had read on the label—4-etioallocholen-3, 6, 17-trione—had caused the positive test.

Piasecki, facing a two-year ban from competition, which would cause him to miss the 2008 Olympics, appealed his case to the North American Court of Arbitration for Sport. He hoped to have his ban shortened so that he could compete in the Olympics. Piasecki claimed that he was "not significantly negligent as he took numerous precautions to avoid taking any Prohibited Substances."[91] Additionally, he claimed that the two-year ban was excessive because "the supplement was legally sold, not a designer steroid he was trying to buy on the black market."[92] He also claimed, "no competitive advantage was sought or obtained from his taking of the 6-OXO [and] he had no intent to dope."[93]

The arbitrator ruled against Piasecki, upholding the two-year ban that would keep the wrestler from realizing his Olympic dream. The arbitrator noted that Piasecki was attempting to gain a competitive advantage by taking the supplement, which negated his claims that he was not trying to dope: "He was not the victim of exceptional circumstances, such as in the case of injury or illness. Rather, he was seeking to improve his recovery time and to increase his testosterone production."[94]

Further, the arbitrator noted that USADA rules impose a "strict liability" standard upon athletes, and that it is well known that athletes bear the ultimate responsibility for what they put into their bodies:

> The fact that the ingredients specifically listed on the 6-OXO label were not themselves listed on the List is only the first level of inquiry to be made when taking supplements. It is known in the sporting community that supplements are unregulated and that numerous athletes have been declared ineligible after mistakenly taking such supplements. Mr. Piasecki's ignorance of this situation is difficult to believe. He could have and should have known about this risk and his personal duty to do more than trust a supplement's ingredient list and/or a supplement sales person.[95]

Piasecki's case, the arbitrator ruled, was unlike cases in which athletes have tested positive after taking supplements that were tainted with a banned substance. Rather, the supplement's label described its effects as raising testosterone and limiting estrogen levels, and one of the main categories on the prohibited list is "Agents with Anti-Estrogenic Activity."[96] The arbitrator noted:

> The 6-OXO label statement regarding estrogen suppression matched the heading of one of the List classes of Prohibited Substances. Thus, with the exercise of ordinary caution, Mr. Piasecki could have suspected that 6-OXO was a Prohibited Substance. He thought he was being cautious based on his own interpretation of the List, when he in fact was taking a great risk in not reading carefully the List and the information

available about a supplement whose label featured the claims "Stimulates Testosterone Production; Suppresses Estrogen Production; Prohormone Alternative." This specifically identified on the label that the product fit squarely into the S4 class of Prohibited Substances: an anti-estrogenic substance.[97]

Dietary supplements are generally safe and effective.

The product that Nathan Piasecki purchased at the Vitamin Shoppe, 6-OXO, was sold legally because it is considered a "dietary supplement" under federal law. A dietary supplement is defined as one of the following:

(A) a vitamin;

(B) a mineral;

(C) an herb or other botanical;

(D) an amino acid;

(E) a dietary substance for use by man to supplement the diet by increasing the total dietary intake; or

(F) a concentrate, metabolite, constituent, extract, or combination of any ingredient described in clause (A), (B), (C), (D), or (E).[98]

Although clauses A through D are fairly specific, clauses E and F are vaguely worded and give manufacturers the opportunity to bring a wide range of substances to the market. Under the Dietary Supplement Health and Education Act (DSHEA), the manufacturing and distribution of dietary supplements are regulated much less stringently than medications. Manufacturers are not required to conduct rigorous safety and effectiveness studies like those required of drug manufacturers, because Congress found that "dietary supplements are safe within a broad range of intake, and safety problems with the supplements are relatively rare."[99] Instead, the U.S. Food and Drug Administration (FDA) is empowered to remove dangerous supplements from the marketplace and to require manufacturers to collect safety and effectiveness data.

Supporters of dietary supplements say that the substances are generally very safe. According to the Natural Products Association (NPA), a trade industry group:

> Dietary supplements have a great safety record, especially compared with other consumer goods, such as drugs and even other foods.... Prescription drugs, for all the testing they go through and copious usage directions that are issued with them, are estimated to be one of the top five leading causes of death in the U.S. at more than 106,000 annually.... More than 5,000 Americans are killed each year by food borne illnesses.... [By contrast,] in 2001, the FDA received 1,214 reports of adverse events regarding dietary supplements. That same year, it received more than 300,000 adverse reports about drugs. So, supplements represent less than half of one percent of drug adverse events using current FDA data.[100]

Many individuals vouch for the effectiveness of dietary supplements, and a number of studies of individual supplements indicate their health benefits. However, because manufacturers of dietary supplements do face strict requirements to demonstrate their effectiveness, consumers are left to make their own decisions. To help consumers make an informed decision, the Office of Dietary Supplements of the National Institutes of Health maintains an online database of research on dietary supplements, called Computer Access to Research on Dietary Supplements (CARDS). The Natural Products Association points out, "Dietary supplements do work, and every week more and more scientific research upholds this fact. There are literally thousands of research articles supporting the efficacy of a wide range of dietary supplements."[101]

Manufacturers are allowed to make claims about the purpose of a dietary supplement, so long as it does not mention a specific disease. For example, a dietary supplement can list its benefits as promoting joint health, but it cannot be touted as a treatment for arthritis. Additionally, any claim of benefits must be accompanied by the following disclaimer: "This statement has not been evaluated by the Food and Drug Administration. This product is not intended to diagnose, treat, cure, or prevent any disease."[102]

Athletes use a wide variety of dietary supplements. Some supplements, such as vitamins and minerals, are relatively uncontroversial. Other legal supplements, however, are banned by sports governing bodies such as USADA, professional leagues, or the National Collegiate Athletic Association (NCAA). The substance Piasecki took is an example. Another well-known example is ephedra, an herbal stimulant that sports governing bodies banned after several athletes who had used the supplement died during strenuous workouts. The FDA, Congress, and state governments have all pursued action to ban ephedra, with several states passing laws and the FDA issuing a nationwide ban that has been challenged in federal court.

Other supplements, although remaining legal under U.S. law and allowed by most sports governing bodies, generate a great deal of debate. Perhaps the most widely debated supplement is creatine, which some studies suggest has the potential to improve athletic performance. For example, one small study[103] examined the effects of three days of creatine use on male and female athletes. The group who took creatine showed increased muscle mass and improved performance in sprints. But the body of evidence on creatine is inconsistent, with some studies showing positive effects, and others showing little to no effect. Studies on side effects are also inconsistent, which makes it difficult for critics to say with authority that creatine is harmful.

It is probably the popularity of creatine—rather than its side effects or benefits—that makes it controversial. In a 2001 study, the NCAA found that 25.8 percent of college athletes had used creatine in the previous year.[104] The NCAA has banned its member institutions from providing creatine and other "muscle-building"[105] supplements to collegiate athletes, although creatine use is not prohibited. Therefore, many athletes purchase their own creatine supplements at health food stores.

Supporters of creatine and other dietary supplements tout the beneficial effects that these substances can have on athletes:

Enforcement Provisions Under DSHEA

The FDA has the authority to declare dietary supplements to be "adulterated" and remove them from the marketplace if the agency can demonstrate that the supplement poses a "significant or unreasonable risk of illness or injury" under normal use.

(f) Dietary supplement or ingredient: safety

(1) [A product is adulterated] if it is a dietary supplement or contains a dietary ingredient that—

(A) presents a significant or unreasonable risk of illness or injury under—

(i)   conditions of use recommended or suggested in labeling, or

(ii) if no conditions of use are suggested or recommended in the labeling, under ordinary conditions of use;

(B) is a new dietary ingredient for which there is inadequate information to provide reasonable assurance that such ingredient does not present a significant or unreasonable risk of illness or injury;

(C) the Secretary declares to pose an imminent hazard to public health or safety, except that the authority to make such declaration shall not be delegated and the Secretary shall promptly after such a declaration initiate a proceeding in accordance with sections 554 and 556 of title 5 to affirm or withdraw the declaration; or

(D) is or contains a dietary ingredient that renders it adulterated under paragraph (a)(1) under the conditions of use recommended or suggested in the labeling of such dietary supplement.

In any proceeding under this subparagraph, the United States shall bear the burden of proof on each element to show that a dietary supplement is adulterated. The court shall decide any issue under this paragraph on a de novo basis.

making the athletes stronger and faster, and therefore making athletic competition more exciting. Unlike steroids and other illegal substances, dietary supplements do not give athletes an unfair advantage or create pressure to ingest dangerous substances, supporters say. Layne Norton, a competitive bodybuilder and nutritional science graduate student dismisses the argument

(2) Before the Secretary may report to a United States attorney a violation of paragraph (1)(A) for a civil proceeding, the person against whom such proceeding would be initiated shall be given appropriate notice and the opportunity to present views, orally and in writing, at least 10 days before such notice, with regard to such proceeding.

The FDA has the power to declare new products "adulterated" if the manufacturer has not submitted evidence that the ingredient's safety can be "reasonably expected":

A dietary supplement which contains a new dietary ingredient shall be deemed adulterated under section [f] unless it meets one of the following requirements:

(1) The dietary supplement contains only dietary ingredients which have been present in the food supply as an article used for food in a form in which the food has not been chemically altered.

(2) There is a history of use or other evidence of safety establishing that the dietary ingredient when used under the conditions recommended or suggested in the labeling of the dietary supplement will reasonably be expected to be safe and, at least 75 days before being introduced or delivered for introduction into interstate commerce, the manufacturer or distributor of the dietary ingredient or dietary supplement provides the Secretary with information, including any citation to published articles, which is the basis on which the manufacturer or distributor has concluded that a dietary supplement containing such dietary ingredient will reasonably be expected to be safe.

Source: Dietary Supplement Health and Education Act, 21 U.S.C., sections 342 and 352(b).

that creatine gives athletes an unfair advantage: "This is a ludicrous claim. Creatine is available to anyone and is very affordable (a 250-day supply can be found for as little as $19.99.)"[106]

Punishing athletes for using legal substances is illogical.

Nathan Piasecki is not the first person to be banned from competing in the Olympics for using a legally purchased substance. Zach Lund was barred from the skeleton competition at the 2006 Winter Olympics. (Skeleton is a sport similar to the luge, but in which sliders race headfirst down the same kind of track used in the luge and bobsled races.) Lund's suspension was the result of testing positive in November 2005 for Propecia, a hair-loss drug that he had been taking for years, but which had recently been banned because it is thought that it can be used to mask steroid use in urine tests. Lund had always listed the drug on forms that he had submitted to USADA, but he had failed to recheck the most recent list of prohibited substances, perhaps having little reason to think that his hair-loss drug could be considered to be giving him a competitive edge.

In January 2006, USADA recognized that Lund had not been trying to engage in any effort to mask steroid use (since he had reported his use of Propecia). They punished him with a public warning and disqualification of his recent results, but declared him eligible to compete at the 2006 Olympics.

WADA appealed USADA's decision to the Court of Arbitration for Sport (CAS). (Although USADA is responsible for determining the eligibility of U.S. athletes, WADA makes its own determinations as to whether an athlete should be eligible for international competition, and can appeal to CAS if it disagrees with a decision by USADA or another nation's anti-doping agency.) In a ruling issued on February 10, 2006—the day of the Winter Olympics opening ceremony—the CAS agreed that Lund had not been trying to cheat and had not gained a competitive advantage by taking Propecia. However, the court ruled that Lund had taken a prohibited substance and therefore must be suspended from competition. Although the court reduced his suspension from two years to one, Lund was sent home from Italy, unable to compete.

Piasecki and Lund both tested positive for substances that were purchased legally and which the athletes did not realize were banned. Other athletes have tested positive after taking legal supplements that were contaminated with substances not listed on the label. Perhaps the best-known case is that of U.S. swimmer Kicker Vencill, who received a two-year ban after taking a multivitamin supplement that contained a banned substance not listed on the supplement's label. Vencill's urine tested positive for 19-norandrosterone, a substance that appears when the banned steroid nandrolone breaks down in the body. Vencill sent the supplements he was taking to a laboratory for testing, and the laboratory concluded that his "Super Complete" vitamin supplement contained three anabolic agents: androstenediol, androstenedione, and norandrostenedione. The CAS upheld Vencill's two-year suspension, noting: "By using supplements while failing to make even the most rudimentary inquiry into their nature, let alone test them to ensure that they were free from contamination, the athlete does not meet the well-established standards required to justify a reduction of his sanction."[107]

Vencill later sued the manufacturer of his vitamins, and after a jury awarded him more than $500,000, Vencill settled with the company for an undisclosed amount rather than have the case go to an appeals court. However, Vencill still lost two years of the prime of his career, based on what many believe to be an unfair standard. Is it really fair to expect an athlete to pay for laboratory testing of every bottle of vitamins that he or she takes?

In a law review article, Jessica Foschi criticizes USADA and WADA's "strict liability" policy for athletes. She writes that the policy that holds athletes liable for positive tests even though they did not deliberately ingest banned substances "takes an individual who is in every other respect a role model and turns them into the disgrace of the sporting world."[108] She dismisses the rationale that the strict liability rule is needed because guilty athletes could blame positive tests upon accidental ingestion of banned substances: "To suspend some innocent athletes so that no guilty athlete ever competes is to belittle the years of preparation, dedication, and commitment to their sport that these athletes have contributed."[109]

Additionally, it could be argued, athletes like Lund, Piasecki, and Vencill, who are taking readily available substances purchased legally, are not the problem. The problem, rather, is athletes like those involved in the BALCO scandal who use black-market "designer" steroids that cannot be detected under current testing. In other words, strict liability to make sure no cheaters escape punishment only makes sense if all cheaters are being caught.

Although many athletes who test positive for steroids have made vague claims that they must have taken tainted supplements, the Mitchell Report helped to discredit such claims. Commenting on the Mitchell Report, the Natural Products Association's David Seckman said:

> The Mitchell report lends substantiation and credibility to what we have been saying for a long time: Dietary supplements have been a convenient and often unquestioned scapegoat to hide illegal steroid use. . . .
>
> The fact that the performance-enhancing substances purchased in the report needed to be obtained surreptitiously by a third party, typically at a high cost, should have been evidence enough to an athlete that the product was likely to be illegal. Clearly, calling such products "dietary supplements" was an attempt to gain legitimacy and mask their real contents.[110]

Current laws regulating dietary supplements are sufficient and should be enforced more vigorously.

Supporters of nutritional supplements—including manufacturers, athletes, health professionals, and ordinary citizens—are continually fending off attacks on the Dietary Supplement Health and Education Act, which critics charge does not do enough to regulate the dietary supplement industry. Supporters of DSHEA, however, argue that supplements are generally safe and manufacturers are generally reputable. Rather than agreeing to further regulation by Congress, they support increasing the FDA's budget for pursuing manufacturers who sell mislabeled or tainted supplements and for keeping supplements with documented risks, such as the stimulant ephedra, off the market.

In March 2006, the House Committee on Government Reform, which has been investigating performance-enhancing drug use in sports on an ongoing basis, held hearings about possible revisions to DSHEA. Congressman Chris Cannon of Utah, a state that is home to many supplement manufacturers, testified that nutritional supplements are important to the health of the people of the United States: "Americans are responsible individuals who should have the freedom to make their own health assessment as to what they do or do not do to promote their health. Many, like myself, take dietary supplements in order to meet their nutritional needs as well as for prevention and health promotion."[111]

Addressing the committee's primary concern that substances that were being marketed as natural alternatives to steroids and sold as dietary supplements did in fact contain illegal steroids, Cannon argued that the answer was not to punish the entire supplement industry. He testified:

> Those who use illegal drugs are committing a crime and should be punished accordingly. Unfortunately, those who

have abused these drugs have tainted the dietary supplement industry, of which millions have achieved better health from. Even the U.S. Food and Drug Administration, the agency that regulates dietary supplements, acknowledges that just because a steroid—or any product—is marketed as a dietary supplement doesn't make it one. As I see it, we don't have a problem with dietary supplement regulation or safety; rather we have a problem with anabolic steroid enforcement. . . .

I believe that consumers are protected under DSHEA, and it is the abuse of a very few corrupt companies that have wrongly implicated a legitimate industry.[112]

In Cannon's view, products that contain steroids are illegal under the Anabolic Steroid Control Act, and the government should punish the sellers of illegal substances. Seckman, of the NPA, made a similar point when commenting on the Mitchell Report:

Just as the Mitchell Report named athletes who were allegedly involved in use of illegal steroids, when an athlete or testing organization claims a dietary supplement is adulterated with illegal substances, the product brand and manufacturer must be named. . . .

Dietary supplements are safe, and Americans should be confident that they are. But when products don't contain what's on their labels or contain something that isn't it demands immediate attention. Consumers, government, and industry need to know who is breaking the rules so we can protect public health.[113]

For products that are truly dietary supplements, Cannon argued, the current system is sufficient to protect consumers:

Under DSHEA, the FDA has the power to seize a supplement if it poses an "unreasonable or significant risk of illness or injury" as well as stop the sale of an entire class of dietary supplements if they pose an imminent public health hazard. DSHEA grants the FDA authority to terminate marketing of a new dietary ingredient if the agency has not received sufficient data in advance.[114]

The main argument against regulating dietary supplements like prescription and nonprescription drugs is that the lengthy testing and approval process for drugs adds tremendously to their cost to consumers and often delays for years the availability of useful medications. Unlike new medications, which are typically synthesized in a laboratory and are unlike anything that human bodies have experienced, dietary supplements are often derived from foods or traditional herbal remedies or are substances that occur naturally in the human body. Thus, a long, drawn-out approval process would be unneeded bureaucracy.

On the other hand, many people, particularly athletes who are tested regularly for banned substances, want some assurances that the supplements they take are pure, contain only the ingredients on the label, and do not contain substances that cause positive results in doping tests. Certainly, Kicker Vencill and Nathan Piasecki could have benefited from such assurances. However, an alternative to ineffective government bureaucracy already exists.

For years, independent private organizations have tested and certified products and given their seals of approval. One example is Underwriters Laboratories (UL), which since 1903 has tested electrical products, tools, and building materials for safety, giving its familiar seal of approval ("UL" enclosed in a circle) to products that meet its standards. Consumers can feel much safer if they buy products with UL approval. NSF International is another independent testing organization upon which consumers can rely for assurances of product quality. Among the products tested by NSF International are dietary supplements. Because of their concern about tainted and questionable supplements causing positive drug tests, the NFL and the NFL

Players Association approached NSF International to establish a program under which NSF would test supplements on the NFL's prohibited list.

NSF later expanded its program to include substances on Major League Baseball's and USADA's prohibited lists, and now offers a "Certified for Sport" seal of approval. Under the program, NSF tests to make sure that supplements contain only those ingredients listed on the label, and that no harmful pesticides, metals, or bacterial contamination is present. NSF also inspects facilities to ensure that good manufacturing practices are followed. To eliminate the possibility of cross-contamination by banned substances, NSF only certifies products made by manufacturers who make no banned substances. If some of the ingredients are made by other manufacturers under contract, then those other manufacturers also must produce no banned substances. In other words, to qualify for the NSF Certified for Sport mark, every ingredient in the supplement must be manufactured in a factory in which no banned substances are made, and every step of the manufacturing process is subject to scrutiny.

Summary

In the crackdown on performance-enhancing drugs in sports, several athletes have been banned from competition because of products they purchased legally. In some cases, the supplements were contaminated by banned substances, while in other cases, the athletes tested positive for ingredients listed on the label. Supporters of dietary supplements say that they are safe and effective, and that punishing athletes for taking substances that they can buy in a health food store makes no sense.

Congress has threatened to put tighter restrictions on the dietary supplement industry, but critics of such proposals say that a few rogue manufacturers who have put illegal ingredients in their products have cast the entire industry in a negative light. Tighter restrictions, they say, would limit everyone's access to health-promoting substances. The answer, they say, is tighter enforcement of drug laws against manufacturers who sell steroids disguised as dietary supplements; increased funding for the FDA to investigate dangerous products; and voluntary collaborations such as the Certified for Sports label created by an independent testing laboratory in collaboration with the NFL.

Dietary Supplements Are Harmful to Athletes and Athletic Competition

In February 2003, 23-year-old Steve Bechler was pursuing his dream of making it in the big leagues. He was struggling to crack the Orioles spring training pitching roster, though, reportedly having trouble with his running drills and maintaining his weight. So the young athlete turned to what he thought was a safe pick-me-up that would also help with weight loss: ephedra.

The team had practice one Sunday, and although it was only February, the day was warm and humid in Ft. Lauderdale, Florida, where the Orioles hold spring training. The oppressive weather, combined with the ephedra (which seems to magnify the effects of heat and humidity on the human body) had disastrous results. Bechler's body temperature reportedly soared to 108 degrees. The body cannot handle such temperatures, and several of Bechler's organs failed. Tragically, he died the next day.

Although other factors—including some previously diagnosed medical conditions—contributed to Bechler's death, the coroner put much of the blame on ephedra.

At the time, the herbal supplement was legal and was not banned by Major League Baseball, although the NFL and the NCAA had banned it. Both the NFL and the NCAA had seen tragic deaths linked to ephedra. Minnesota Viking Korey Stringer and Northwestern University's Rashidi Wheeler both collapsed and died during hot, humid conditions in August 2001. Ephedra was found in Stringer's locker and in Wheeler's system.

Baseball, always seeming to lag behind other sports, did not ban ephedra for major leaguers, although it did impose a ban on ephedra for nonunionized minor league players soon after Bechler's death. However, on February 6, 2004, just under a year after Bechler's death, the FDA announced a nationwide ban on ephedra sales.

Taking dietary supplements is risky and not necessary for athletic performance.

Certain dietary supplements, such as ephedra and androstenedione have been singled out for prohibition by sports governing bodies and then the federal government, but most dietary supplements remain largely unregulated.

Sports governing bodies have a variety of attitudes toward dietary supplements, ranging from cautious approval to mild disapproval. For example, the NCAA bans only a few legal dietary supplements, but prohibits schools from distributing to athletes anything other than carbohydrate and electrolyte replacement supplements. Instead of dietary supplements, the NCAA endorses healthy and balanced diets. In the organization's *Sports Medicine Handbook,* Guideline 2g covers dietary supplements and suggests that even relatively harmless supplements such as vitamins and minerals are typically unnecessary, stating, "Most scientific evidence shows that selected vitamins and minerals will not enhance performance provided no deficiency exists."[115]

The organization's official position is that dietary supplements geared specifically toward athletic performance simply do not work: "Many other 'high-tech' nutritional or dietary supplements may seem to be effective at first, but this is likely a placebo effect—if student-athletes believe these substances will enhance performance, they may train harder or work more efficiently. Ultimately, most nutritional supplements are ineffective, costly, and unnecessary."[116]

Nathan Piasecki, the elite wrestler who was suspended for using a substance that he had purchased at a health food store, stopped taking supplements after being banned from competition for two years. In an interview for USADA's newsletter for athletes, Piasecki noted that he did not miss taking supplements. He said, "I never noticed any athletic benefits from taking supplements. Before my positive test, I thought that they were helping me. However, now that I have discontinued their use, I continue to train at the same level and intensity without a decline in my performance."[117]

Even though there is no consensus that dietary supplements actually improve athletic performance, many people feel that the very attempt to boost performance by taking dietary supplements is a form of cheating because it is an attempt to gain an unnatural advantage. In Piasecki's case, the USADA argued, "Though Mr. Piasecki claims that he did not seek a competitive advantage, it is clear what the product was intended to do, which was to generate testosterone to increase muscle mass. Mr. Piasecki testified he took it to aid in recovery. Mr. Piasecki was using the supplement and obtaining a competitive advantage over non-using athletes."[118]

Athletes must be responsible about what they put into their bodies.

Some have argued that there must be some sort of "safe haven" for athletes to take legal supplements, perhaps by reducing or eliminating penalties for athletes who can prove that positive doping tests were caused by tainted supplements, or athletes who innocently took a legal substance that they did not realize was banned. Anti-doping advocates, however, believe that a "strict liability" standard is necessary.

One problem with relaxing the standard is that supplements create an easy excuse for athletes who use performance-enhancing drugs. Mike Cameron, upon being suspended by Major League Baseball for using a banned stimulant, said, "I can only conclude that a nutritional supplement I was taking was tainted. Unfortunately, the actual supplement is gone and therefore cannot be tested."[119] Other high-profile athletes including NFL linebacker Shawne Merriman, baseball player Rafael Palmeiro, and shot-putter C.J. Hunter, plus countless others, have used the "tainted supplement" defense.

Sports governing bodies, however, rarely take this defense seriously. It might be possible to prove that a supplement contains a banned substance, but how can an athlete prove that he or she was not using that banned substance deliberately?

Supplements also give athletes a means to explain away the huge increases in muscle size and improvements in athletic performance associated with performance-enhancing drug use. In his book *Steroid Nation*, Shaun Assael uses the example of NFL linebacker Bill "Romo" Romanowski. While with the Broncos, he showed up for the Super Bowl with a tackle box full of products from supplement maker EAS. When the Broncos dominated the game, Assael suggests, viewers "got the message that Romo's tackle box had helped to work a miracle. It would take months for evidence to emerge that Romanowski was also on steroids and human growth hormone."[120]

Mark McGwire caused a similar sensation with androstenedione, or "andro," when a reporter pointed out a bottle of it in McGwire's locker and McGwire attributed his power increase to using the substance, which was legal at the time. His claims helped andro sales skyrocket. (It was subsequently outlawed by the Anabolic Steroid Control Act of 2004.) Jose Canseco, however,

Federal Court Upholds Ephedra Ban

After the FDA issued a ban on ephedra in early 2004, dietary supplement manufacturer Nutraceutical Corporation challenged the ban in court, arguing that the FDA had acted improperly in completely banning ephedra without making an exception for low-dose supplements. At the local level, the federal court sided with Nutraceutical Corporation, but the government appealed the ruling. The U.S. Court of Appeals for the 10th Circuit reversed the lower court and reinstated the ban. The panel noted that the FDA had received numerous reports linking ephedra to heart attacks, strokes, seizures, and deaths during the 1980s and 1990s and had first attempted to issue a ban on ephedra in 1996:

> In determining that [ephedrine-alkaloid dietary supplements (EDS)] pose an "unreasonable risk of illness or injury," the FDA found that the weight loss and other health benefits possible from the use of EDS were dwarfed by the potential long-term harm to the user's cardiovascular system. The agency went on to enact a complete ban on the product after making a finding that any amount of EDS had negative ramifications on the cardiovascular system and, based on the FDA's analysis, EDS provided no benefits so great as to justify such risk.
>
> The preponderance of the evidence standard requires the party with the burden of proof to support its position with the greater weight of the evidence.... The evidence relied on by the FDA to enact its ban of EDS covers over seven years of agency review, public notice and comment, peer-reviewed literature, and scientific data. It is the purview of the FDA to weigh the evidence, including the evidence submitted by Nutraceutical and other manufacturers during public notice and comment....
>
> The FDA's extensive research identified the dose level at which ephedrine alkaloids present unreasonable risk of illness or injury to be so minuscule that no amount of EDS is reasonably safe. The FDA reasonably concluded that there is no recommended dose of EDS that does not present an unreasonable risk.... The FDA was not arbitrary or capricious in its Final Rule; the FDA met its statutory burden of justifying a total ban of EDS by a preponderance of the evidence.

Source: *Nutraceutical Corporation v. Von Eschenbach*, 459 F.3d 1033 (10th Cir., 2006), cert. denied, May 14, 2007.

accused McGwire of using andro as a cover-up for his steroid use. Canseco suggested: "If you're taking steroids, you don't need androstenedione. . . . I don't believe Mark McGwire was even taking andro. . . . I'm virtually certain that Mark created the andro controversy as a distraction."[121]

As Kicker Vencill's case illustrates, some supplements are indeed tainted with banned substances. However, anti-doping advocates firmly believe that the answer to this problem is not to excuse the athlete who takes a tainted supplement, but to admonish the athlete who takes supplements despite the well-publicized risk of contamination and the many official warnings by sports governing bodies. As the Court of Arbitration for Sport noted in the *Vencill* case:

> Without wishing to attribute any particular motivation to Mr. Vencill in this case, we hold that for an athlete in this day and age to rely—as this athlete claims he did—on the advice of friends and on product labels when deciding to use supplements and vitamins, is tantamount to a type of willful blindness for which he must be held responsible. This "see no evil, hear no evil, speak no evil" attitude in the face of what rightly has been called the scourge of doping in sport—this failure to exercise the slightest caution in the circumstances—is not only unacceptable and to be condemned, it is a far cry from the attitude and conduct expected of an athlete seeking the mitigation of his sanction for a doping violation.[122]

In addition to the danger that supplements might not be what their manufacturers purport them to be, some argue that muscle-building supplements are a "gateway" to the use of steroids and other performance-enhancing drugs. (Similar arguments are used about cigarettes being a gateway to illegal drug use and marijuana being a gateway to "harder" drugs such as heroin.) John McCloskey and Julian Bailes suggest that athletes "are dealing with increasing incentive to succeed and growing pressure to do what is necessary to stay competitive, [and they] are choosing to cheat. They see the progression from supplements to steroids as justifiable and unavoidable."[123]

Current laws regulating dietary supplements are too weak.

Supporters of the dietary supplement industry say that a few "rogue" manufacturers are making the industry look bad by selling muscle-building products that contain undisclosed ingredients that are steroids or steroid-related compounds. Opponents of the industry counter that the current regulatory structure makes it too easy for manufacturers to get away with selling tainted supplements because manufacturers are not required to submit their products to the FDA for testing before they go to market. Rather, supplement manufacturers put products containing steroids into the marketplace, and people who use them note muscle gains caused by the steroids, making them repeat customers and spreading the word to other potential buyers. Referring to the Utah lawmaker who championed the 1994 law regulating supplements, Assael notes, "If Senator Orrin Hatch wanted to slow down the doping fight, he couldn't have done better than pushing a bill like DSHEA."[124]

While supporters of DSHEA argue that the FDA has authority to remove dangerous dietary supplements from the marketplace, opponents point out that supplement manufacturers have few obstacles to getting their products into the marketplace. The FDA, on the other hand, faces greater obstacles to getting products out of the marketplace. Janell Mayo Duncan of Consumers Union, the nonprofit organization that publishes *Consumer Reports* magazine, pointed out some of the objections to DSHEA:

> DSHEA created serious regulatory loopholes that have opened the floodgates to thousands of untested dietary supplement

products. Benefits and risks do not have to be established before these products are brought to market. Manufacturers are not required to disclose when new products cause harm, and the law requires the FDA to first prove that a supplement creates a significant or unreasonable risk before it can demand its removal from the market. . . . There are a significant growing number of questionable products that likely would not be allowed on the market if they were subject to pre-market safety testing. Because there are no requirements that a dietary supplement be proven safe and effective before going on the market, it is very difficult for consumers to determine which products are safe and worth consuming and which are ineffective and/or dangerous.[125]

She discussed the many years that it took for the FDA to ban ephedra, during which time more than 100 deaths and 17,000 health problems, including heart attacks and strokes, were linked to the herbal supplement. Even after the ban, court challenges slowed its implementation. Mayo Duncan outlined some of the changes that Consumers Union felt were necessary to strengthen the law:

- Requiring an expert panel to review the safety of dietary supplement products on the market

- Requiring dietary supplement manufacturers to tell the FDA when they become aware of serious adverse events associated with the use of their products

- Premarket testing requirements for certain supplements

- Product ingredient registration

- Risk labeling requirements.[126]

Even when products are exposed as containing steroid-related compounds, pulling the products off the market is not easy or quick. In July 2006, the FDA sent an official "Warning Letter" to bodybuilding.com, notifying the company that 6-OXO and other muscle-building supplements sold on the Web site were considered "adulterated" because they contained substances not traditionally found in food or traditionally available as dietary supplements, and because the FDA had received no information about the safety or effectiveness of the products.[127]

It was months later, in January 2007, that Nathan Piasecki's use of the product 6-OXO, which was marketed as a dietary supplement, caused him to test positive in a test for performance-enhancing drugs. During Piasecki's hearing, the director of the drug-testing laboratory at the University of California, Los Angeles (UCLA), USADA's premier laboratory, testified under oath that 6-OXO is an anabolic steroid. Yet, almost two years after 6-OXO caught the FDA's attention, the supplement remained widely available, and its manufacturer, Ergopharm, continued to market it as "drug free, legal, and effective."[128]

Unfortunately, some say, the vague wording of DSHEA allows manufacturers to market just about anything as a dietary supplement. McCloskey and Bailes write, "Even if [athletes] don't cross over from legal supplements to illegal drugs, the line they step up to by taking most supplements becomes a little more blurred every day."[129] Criticizing steroid-like supplements, they write, "If it looks like a steroid, works like a steroid (in gaining quick, substantial mass and strength), and has the side effects identical to those of steroids, then what else is it?"[130]

Summary

With a few notable exceptions, dietary supplements remain largely unregulated by the government under DSHEA. The FDA banned ephedra under the law's authority, and "andro" was reclassified as an illegal steroid by the Anabolic Steroid Control Act, a subsequent law. Sports governing bodies ban additional substances that are still sold legally as dietary supplements, but supplement manufacturers still take advantage of weak regulation and enforcement by marketing "dietary supplements" that are really steroids.

Anti-doping advocates have called on Congress to tighten regulation of dietary supplements, and sports governing bodies have taken a hard-line approach while waiting for Congress to act. Generally, athletes are subjected to a "strict liability" rule, holding them responsible for what they put in their bodies. Although the rule has resulted in some seemingly unfair results, athletes can avoid trouble by staying away from supplements, which many say are not that helpful and certainly not worth the risk.

The Future of Doping

As Major League Baseball teams reported for spring training in 2008, it was not clear which direction the anti-doping fight was heading. On the one hand, baseball had seen many of its stars held up to public scorn, with Barry Bonds under indictment for perjury and still hoping to catch on with a new team after being kicked off the Giants. Roger Clemens was facing a perjury probe, and Andy Pettite had admitted to HGH use. Congress was still parading MLB, NFL, NHL, and NBA officials in front of committees and asking dramatic questions as the TV cameras rolled.

On the other hand, the sports leagues had a valid argument that most of the problems that had plagued baseball had been the result of the slow response to the problem. The leagues argued that they were taking the problem seriously. In general, Americans seemed to want Congress to stay out of the business of steroid testing. However, the one glaring issue hanging over the major American sports was testing for HGH, which would require overcoming the players' unions' long-standing opposition to blood testing.

The Beginning of Widespread HGH Testing?

Although the country's sports leagues are catching up to international standards, it seems as if the cheaters are always a step ahead of the people trying to catch them. As was the case with EPO and BALCO, athletes were taking substances that they knew would not show up in drug tests. The widespread availability of HGH, coupled with the absence of a reliable test, caused an unknown but presumably large number of athletes to use the substance. Athletes at the 2004 and 2006 Olympics were given HGH tests, but the tests were not very sensitive, and athletes could easily beat the test by discontinuing use a few days before the test. Only a limited number of athletes were tested, and year-round testing was not possible because the chemicals needed for the test were not being mass-produced. The result was that no athletes tested positive for HGH at the 2004 and 2006 games. "We know people have been taking human growth hormone with impunity and have been for 20 years,"[131] lamented one WADA official.

Prior to the 2008 Olympics in Beijing, WADA officials promised that a reliable HGH test would be available in time to protect the integrity of the games. They announced that they would be addressing both of the problems that had troubled officials in previous years, by mass-producing test kits that could detect HGH beyond the 48-hour window of the existing tests. WADA's HGH test requires a blood sample, because, as the organization's Web site notes, "In the view of international scientific experts, efforts to develop a reliable urine test for HGH would require significant resources and time, and chances of success appear remote."[132]

Of course, the problem of HGH use has already been established among American professional athletes, with numerous athletes and team employees linked to HGH through criminal

Major league discrepancies for illegal drug and steroid tests

Testing policies for drugs – illegal steroids, masking agents and recreational drugs – differ widely in U.S. sports leagues. Major League Baseball's new mandatory testing plan appears to give cheating players every advantage to avoid detection.

	Major League Baseball	National Basketball Association	National Football League	National Hockey League	International Olympic Committee
Testing	All players will be tested for illegal steroids during spring training and the regular season. There is no off-season testing.	Rookies are tested up to four times per season for steroids and recreational drugs, while veterans are subject to one random test during training camp.	Players are randomly tested year-round for steroids, and annually for recreational drugs. Both are banned.	There is no mandatory drug-testing policy. The only drug testing is for players already in the league's substance abuse aftercare program.	Athletes are subject to in- and out-of-competition random testing at both national and international events.
Penalties	First violation: player is placed in a treatment program. Second: 15-day suspension or $10,000 fine. Third: 25-day suspension or $25,000 fine. Fourth: 50-day suspension or $50,000 fine. Fifth: One-year suspension or $100,000 fine.	First violation for steroids: five-game suspension and entry into a treatment program. Second: ten-game suspension and treatment program. Third: 25-game suspension and treatment program. Players who test positive for narcotic recreational drugs are dismissed and disqualified.	Suspensions are mandatory for positive steroid tests – four games for the first offense, six games for the second and at least a year for the third. Recreational drug users are suspended if they fail a follow-up test.	Players who are abusers can seek help the first time without being exposed or suspended.	Automatic disqualification from event for any banned substance and loss of medals. Two-year suspension for the first violation; lifetime ban for second violation.

SOURCE: Associated Press   AP

The graphic above compares the drug policies of major U.S. sports leagues and the Olympics. The NHL recently followed the example set by the other leagues and instituted mandatory testing in 2005.

investigations. However, the players' unions have never consented to blood tests, which would be required for HGH testing. It will be interesting to see whether members of Congress will use the players' unions' refusal as leverage to finally pass comprehensive drug testing like that proposed in bills that have failed over the past several years. Already, in reaction to the number of athletes and ordinary citizens who have gotten HGH from questionable clinics, legislators have introduced legislation to make

HGH a controlled substance. This means that prescriptions for it would be regulated much more closely.

Doping and the Hall of Fame

Some of baseball's premier sluggers have been accused of steroid use, along with pitching legend Roger "the Rocket" Clemens. Based on numbers alone, Mark McGwire, Sammy Sosa, Barry Bonds, and Clemens would certainly be headed for the Baseball Hall of Fame in Cooperstown, New York. However, voters are supposed to also consider a player's character and conduct. All-time hits leader Pete Rose is still fighting to get into the Hall of Fame, having been banished from the game for betting on baseball. Some have questioned whether anyone who has been linked to performance-enhancing drugs should also be kept out of Cooperstown.

When McGwire first became eligible for the Hall of Fame in 2007, sports journalists publicly debated whether he deserved to be voted in. Ultimately, fewer than 1 in 4 voters (primarily baseball writers) selected McGwire on their ballots, far short of the 75 percent needed for election. At the time, many speculated that voters were simply trying to send a message by not electing McGwire in his first year of eligibility, especially when Tony Gwynn and Cal Ripken Jr., two players known for their character were being inducted. However, McGwire received the exact same number of votes in 2008, when fiery relief pitcher Rich "Goose" Gossage was the only player elected. Some have begun to question whether McGwire and Sosa will ever make it to the Hall of Fame, even though a February 2008 Gallup Poll found that 68 percent of people identifying themselves as baseball fans thought that Sosa should be elected to the Hall of Fame, with 61 percent supporting McGwire.[133]

When it comes to Barry Bonds, however, his numbers might simply be too good to ignore. Many have argued that he was on track to be in the Hall of Fame—based on his batting average, fielding ability, and stolen bases—before he was alleged to have begun using steroids. "People forget this guy was a Hall of Fame player when he was a skinny kid for the Pittsburgh Pirates. He was the greatest player in the 1990s, and you can argue that he is the greatest player in baseball history,"[134] one baseball writer said.

The only question is whether voters will look past the cloud hanging over the latter stages of Bonds's career. The secretary

Proposed Bill Restricting Human Growth Hormone Distribution

With revelations that a number of athletes had obtained human growth hormone (HGH), with and without prescriptions, lawmakers proposed making HGH a controlled substance. Under the federal Controlled Substances Act, doctors must follow strict procedures in writing prescriptions and keeping records of prescriptions for controlled substances. Furthermore, possession of controlled substances without a valid prescription is a crime. Athletes seeking to use HGH would either have to obtain the substance illegally or leave a paper trail of prescriptions that would allow league officials to uncover the use of the banned substance. The bill was introduced in 2007 and must pass both houses of Congress and be signed by the president to become law.

SECTION 1. SHORT TITLE.
This Act may be cited as the "Human Growth Hormone Restriction Act of 2007."

SEC. 2. HUMAN GROWTH HORMONE.
(a) In General: Schedule III of section 202(c) of the Controlled Substances Act (21 U.S.C. 812(c)) is amended by adding at the end the following:
  (f) Growth hormone, recombinant human growth hormone, or human growth hormone.
(b) Effective Date: The amendment made by this section shall take effect 60 days after the date of enactment of this Act.

Source: Human Growth Hormone Restriction Act of 2007, H.R. 4911, 110th Congress, 1st Session (2007).

of the baseball writers group responsible for tabulating Hall of Fame votes told the *San Francisco Chronicle*, "As someone who has been counting ballots for 13 years, I can say our people don't like drug users,"[135] referring to two players with impressive career statistics but who failed to make the Hall of Fame after admitting to cocaine use. The case against performance-enhancing drug users, whose statistics are tainted, would seem to be much stronger than the case against recreational drug users.

Government Prosecution of High-profile Athletes

On March 8, 2008, former world-class sprinter Marion Jones, who at one time might have been the most celebrated female athlete in the world, reported to prison to begin serving a six-month sentence. She had pleaded guilty to perjury (lying under oath) during the government's investigation of the BALCO probe. On the day that she surrendered, Barry Bonds faced a similar perjury indictment for lying to the BALCO grand jury. Also around that same time, a Congressional committee requested that the FBI investigate whether Roger Clemens could be charged with perjury for his testimony before the committee the previous month, in which he denied sworn allegations by his former trainer that the trainer had injected the pitcher with steroids and HGH.

Some questioned the fairness of the whole process. Although Jones agreed to a six-month sentence, the man at the center of the whole BALCO mess, Victor Conte, served only four months. Some have accused the federal government with being obsessed with exposing star athletes as drug users, notably the federal agent who doggedly has pursued Bonds for years. On the one hand, exposing high-profile athletes as cheaters can be a useful tool for helping educate young people about the consequences of drug use.

On the other hand, it could be argued that the government is only singling out high-profile athletes even though the problem of doping is widespread. Star athletes in situations such as appearing before Congress, in which they must testify under oath, face a dilemma. If they deny use, they can face perjury charges, but if they admit use or refuse to answer questions, they face public ridicule. When only high-profile athletes—and not the thousands of others who might be doping—face such scrutiny, they can argue that the government is not playing fair. When the Mitchell Report provided some insight into the widespread nature of performance-enhancing drug use in baseball, *Salon* editor-in-chief Joan Walsh wrote, "The [media's] glaring focus on Bonds was unfair, given what we now know (and baseball insiders have long known) about the prevalence of steroids in the game."[136]

Summary

The BALCO scandal, the Mitchell Report, and the subsequent prosecutions of star athletes for lying about performance-enhancing drug use has gotten the attention of Americans and the people who run the country's popular professional sports leagues. While anti-doping efforts in the Olympics and other international competitions have been getting more stringent, the cheaters always seem to be a step ahead of the testers. Testing for HGH has the potential to take away the cheater's latest weapon, but it is difficult to say how long performance-enhancing drug use can be kept at bay.

Today's athlete lives in a fishbowl, and drug testing gives the public even more insight into athletes' private lives. As testing becomes more rigid, it is only a matter of time before more stars' reputations are sullied. The public loves sports and spends more and more money on live events, merchandise, and television packages. It is difficult to predict, however, whether today's athletes will be remembered with the same reverence as Babe Ruth, Jackie Robinson, Jesse Owens, Muhammad Ali, Michael Jordan, Wayne Gretzky, and Wilma Rudolph.

Beginning Legal Research

The goals of each book in the Point-Counterpoint series are not only to give the reader a basic introduction to a controversial issue affecting society, but also to encourage the reader to explore the issue more fully. This Appendix is meant to serve as a guide to the reader in researching the current state of the law as well as exploring some of the public policy arguments as to why existing laws should be changed or new laws are needed.

Although some sources of law can be found primarily in law libraries, legal research has become much faster and more accessible with the advent of the Internet. This Appendix discusses some of the best starting points for free access to laws and court decisions, but surfing the Web will uncover endless additional sources of information. Before you can research the law, however, you must have a basic understanding of the American legal system.

The most important source of law in the United States is the Constitution. Originally enacted in 1787, the Constitution outlines the structure of our federal government, as well as setting limits on the types of laws that the federal government and state governments can enact. Through the centuries, a number of amendments have added to or changed the Constitution, most notably the first 10 amendments, which collectively are known as the "Bill of Rights" and which guarantee important civil liberties.

Reading the plain text of the Constitution provides little information. For example, the Constitution prohibits "unreasonable searches and seizures" by the police. To understand concepts in the Constitution, it is necessary to look to the decisions of the U.S. Supreme Court, which has the ultimate authority in interpreting the meaning of the Constitution. For example, the U.S. Supreme Court's 2001 decision in Kyllo v. United States held that scanning the outside of a person's house using a heat sensor to determine whether the person is growing marijuana is an unreasonable search—if it is done without first getting a search warrant from a judge. Each state also has its own constitution and a supreme court that is the ultimate authority on its meaning.

Also important are the written laws, or "statutes," passed by the U.S. Congress and the individual state legislatures. As with constitutional provisions, the U.S. Supreme Court and the state supreme courts are the ultimate authorities in interpreting the meaning of federal and state laws, respectively. However, the U.S. Supreme Court might find that a state law violates the U.S. Constitution, and a state supreme court might find that a state law violates either the state or U.S. Constitution.

123

Not every controversy reaches either the U.S. Supreme Court or the state supreme courts, however. Therefore, the decisions of other courts are also important. Trial courts hear evidence from both sides and make a decision, while appeals courts review the decisions made by trial courts. Sometimes rulings from appeals courts are appealed further to the U.S. Supreme Court or the state supreme courts.

Lawyers and courts refer to statutes and court decisions through a formal system of citations. Use of these citations reveals which court made the decision or which legislature passed the statute, and allows one to quickly locate the statute or court case online or in a law library. For example, the Supreme Court case Brown v. Board of Education has the legal citation 347 U.S. 483 (1954). At a law library, this 1954 decision can be found on page 483 of volume 347 of the U.S. Reports, which are the official collection of the Supreme Court's decisions. On the following page, you will find sample of all the major kinds of legal citation.

Finding sources of legal information on the Internet is relatively simple thanks to "portal" sites such as findlaw.com and lexisone.com, which allow the user to access a variety of constitutions, statutes, court opinions, law review articles, news articles, and other useful sources of information. For example, findlaw.com offers access to all Supreme Court decisions since 1893. Other useful sources of information include gpo.gov, which contains a complete copy of the U.S. Code, and thomas.loc.gov, which offers access to bills pending before Congress, as well as recently passed laws. Of course, the Internet changes every second of every day, so it is best to do some independent searching.

Of course, many people still do their research at law libraries, some of which are open to the public. For example, some state governments and universities offer the public access to their law collections. Law librarians can be of great assistance, as even experienced attorneys need help with legal research from time to time.

Common Citation Forms

Source of Law	Sample Citation	Notes
U.S. Supreme Court	*Employment Division v. Smith*, 485 U.S. 660 (1988)	The U.S. Reports is the official record of Supreme Court decisions. There is also an unofficial Supreme Court ("S. Ct.") reporter.
U.S. Court of Appeals	*United States v. Lambert,* 695 F.2d 536 (11th Cir.1983)	Appellate cases appear in the Federal Reporter, designated by "F." The 11th Circuit has jurisdiction in Alabama, Florida, and Georgia.
U.S. District Court	*Carillon Importers, Ltd. v. Frank Pesce Group, Inc.,* 913 F.Supp. 1559 (S.D.Fla.1996)	Federal trial-level decisions are reported in the Federal Supplement ("F. Supp."). Some states have multiple federal districts; this case originated in the Southern District of Florida.
U.S. Code	Thomas Jefferson Commemoration Commission Act, 36 U.S.C., §149 (2002)	Sometimes the popular names of legislation—names with which the public may be familiar—are included with the U.S. Code citation.
State Supreme Court	*Sterling v. Cupp*, 290 Ore. 611, 614, 625 P.2d 123, 126 (1981)	The Oregon Supreme Court decision is reported in both the state's reporter and the Pacific regional reporter.
State Statute	Pennsylvania Abortion Control Act of 1982, 18 Pa. Cons. Stat. 3203-3220 (1990)	States use many different citation formats for their statutes.

Cases and Statutes

Anabolic Steroid Control Act of 2004, Pub. L. no. 108–358, 108th Congress, 2d session (2004)
Federal law reclassifying numerous steroids and related substances as controlled substances, with increased penalties for possession and distribution.

Chandler v. Miller, **520 U.S. 305 (1997)**
U.S. Supreme Court ruling that candidates for public office could not be subjected to drug testing without grounds for suspicion.

Dietary Supplement Health and Education Act, Public Law No. 103–417, 103d Congress, 2d Session (1994)
Federal law giving manufacturers great flexibility in marketing dietary supplements, so long as there is some support for the safety of a product in question.

Flood v. Kuhn, **407 U.S. 258 (1972)**
U.S. Supreme Court case involving player contracts, noting that Congress traditionally has not interfered in the business of professional baseball.

National Labor Relations Act, 29 U.S.C., secs. 151–169.
Federal law giving labor unions (such as those representing professional athletes) the ability to collectively negotiate the conditions of employment.

Nutraceutical Corporation v. Von Eschenbach, **459 F.3d 1033 (10th Cir. 2006)**
Federal appeals court upheld the FDA's ban of supplements containing the herbal stimulant ephedra.

Shoemaker v. Handel, **795 F.2d 1136 (3d Cir. 1986)**
Federal appeals court upheld testing of racehorse jockeys, on the grounds that the state strictly regulated the industry to protect the betting public.

Skinner v. Railway Labor Executives' Association, **489 U.S. 602, 624 (1989)**
U.S. Supreme Court upheld law requiring railroads to run drug tests on employees involved in accidents.

Treasury Employees v. Von Raab, **489 U.S. 656 (1989)**
U.S. Supreme Court upheld drug testing of customs agents who carry weapons or work in drug interdiction.

U.S. v. Comprehensive Drug Testing, **473 F.3d 915 (9th Cir. 2006)**
Federal appeals court upheld the federal government's seizure of computer records of the results of drug tests conducted on Major League Baseball players and other athletes.

U.S. Anti-Doping Agency v. Landis, **AAA No. 30 190 00847 06, North American Court of Arbitration for Sport Panel (20 Sept. 2007)**
Arbitration panel upheld the suspension of American cyclist Floyd Landis for failing a drug test during the Tour de France.

***U.S. Anti-Doping Agency v. Piasecki*, AAA No. 30 190 00358 07, North American Court of Arbitration for Sport Panel (24 Sept. 2007)**
Arbitration panel upheld the suspension of a wrestler who took a substance that was not specifically listed on the prohibited list but clearly fell into a category of prohibited substances.

***Vencill v. U.S. Anti-Doping Agency*, Court of Arbitration for Sport (11 March 2004)**
Arbitration panel upheld the suspension of an American swimmer who blamed his positive doping test on multivitamin supplements, which proved to be contaminated with steroidal compounds.

***Vernonia School Dist. 47J v. Acton*, 515 U.S. 646 (1995)**
U.S. Supreme Court upheld random drug testing of high school athletes.

Terms and Concepts

anabolic steroids
antitrust laws
blood doping
collective bargaining
controlled substances
dietary supplements
doping
expectation of privacy
gateway drug
hormones
human growth hormone (HGH)
masking agent
search and seizure
special needs doctrine
stimulants
strict liability
testosterone
testosterone-to-epitestosterone ratio

NOTES ||||▷

Point: The Media Has Blown the "Problem" of Performance-enhancing Drugs out of Proportion

1 Paul Ledewski, "Ripken, Gwynn Votes Won't Be Unanimous," *Southtown Star*, January 8, 2007, http://www.southtownstar.com/sports/ladewski/201907,081LAD2.article.

2 *Ibid.*

3 Associated Press, "Pound: As many as a third of NHL players may use steroids," *USA Today*, November 24, 2005, http://www.usatoday.com/sports/hockey/nhl/2005–11–24-pound-nhl_x.htm.

4 *Ibid.*

5 Senate Committee on Commerce, Science, and Transportation, *The Clean Sports Act of 2005*, and S. 1334, *The Professional Sports Integrity and Accountability Act*, Senate hearing 109–525, 109th Congress, 1st Session (September 28, 2005).

6 *Ibid.*

7 Jose Canseco, *Juiced: Wild Times, Rampant 'Roids, Smash Hits, and How Baseball Got Big* (New York: Regan Books, 2005), 277.

8 Mike Puma, "Not the Size of the Dog in the Fight," Sportscentury Biography, http://espn.go.com/classic/biography/s/Alzado_Lyle.html.

9 C. Street, J. Antonio, and D. Cudlipp, "Androgen Use by Athletes: A Re-evaluation of the Health Risks," *Canadian Journal of Applied Physiology* 21, no. 6 (1996): 421–440 (abstract).

10 C.M. Colker, J. Antonio, and D. Kalman, "The Metabolism of Orally Ingested 19-Nor-4-Androstene-3,17-dione and 19-Nor-4-Androstene-3,17-diol in Healthy, Resistance-Trained Men," *Journal of Strength and Conditioning Research* 15, no. 1 (2001): 144–147 (abstract).

11 Dayn Perry, "Pumped-Up Hysteria," *Reason* (January 2003), http://www.reason.com/news/show/28645.html.

12 Canseco, *Juiced*, 179.

13 Senate Committee, *The Clean Sports Act of 2005*.

14 *Ibid.*

15 *Ibid.*

16 Dave Goldberg, "Upshaw Says Players Will Accept HGH Testing," *Honolulu Advertiser*, February 1, 2008, http://the.honoluluadvertiser.com/article/2008/Feb/01/br/br7196504823.html/?print=on.

17 *U.S. v. Comprehensive Drug Testing*, 473 F.3d 915 (9th Cir. 2006).

Counterpoint: Performance-enhancing Drugs Are Damaging the Integrity of Athletic Competition

18 Mark Fainaru-Wada and Lance Williams, *Game of Shadows: Barry Bonds, BALCO, and the Steroids Scandal that Rocked Professional Sports* (New York: Gotham Books, 2006), 277.

19 Mike Fish, "Steroid Problem Reaches Critical Mass in the D.R.," ESPN.com, February 14, 2007, http://sports.espn.go.com/espn/print?id=2763194&type=story.

20 *Ibid.*

21 Senate Committee on Commerce, Science, and Transportation, *Steroid Use in Professional Baseball and Anti-Doping Issues in Amateur Sports*, 107th Congress, 2nd Session, June 18, 2002, 34.

22 World Anti-Doping Agency, *Tour de France 2003: Independent Observer Report* (Montreal, Quebec: World Anti-Doping Association, 2003), 13–14.

23 *Ibid.*, 17.

24 Shaun Assael, *Steroid Nation: Juiced Home Run Totals, Anti-Aging Miracles, and a Hercules in Every High School: The Secret Story of America's True Drug Addiction* (New York: ESPN Books, 2007), 213.

25 *Ibid.*

26 House Committee on Government Reform, *Restoring Faith in America's Pastime: Evaluating Major League Baseball's Efforts to Eradicate Steroid Use*, 109th Congress, 1st Session, March 17, 2005, 211.

27 *Ibid.*, 256.

28 Senate Committee, *Steroid Use in Professional Baseball*, 47.

29 George J. Mitchell, *Report to the Commissioner of Baseball of an Independent*

Investigation into the Illegal Use of Ste-roids and Other Performance Enhancing Substances by Players in Major League Baseball, December 13, 2007, 305.

30 Mitchell report, 310.

31 Mitchell report, 288.

32 Drug Enforcement Administration, *Ana-bolic Steroids, A Dangerous and Illegal Way to Seek Athletic Dominance and Bet-ter Appearance* (Washington, D.C.: U.S. Department of Justice, 2004), 3–4.

33 House Committee on Oversight and Government Reform, *Myths and Facts About Human Growth Hormone, B12, and Other Substances*, 110th Congress, 2nd Session (February 12, 2008), testi-mony transcript, 3.

34 House Committee on Commerce and Energy, *Steroids in Sports: Cheating the System and Gambling Your Health*, 109th Congress, 1st Session (March 10, 2005), 12–13.

35 Senate Committee, *Steroid Use in Profes-sional Baseball*, 42.

36 House Committee, *Restoring Faith in America's Pastime*, 119.

Point: Congressional Action on Performance-enhancing Drug Use Is Improper

37 *Flood v. Kuhn,* 407 U.S. 258 (1972).

38 ABC News/ESPN Poll, "Broad Concern about Steroids Fuels Support for Puni-tive Rules," March 16, 2005.

39 *Ibid.*

40 Jack Cafferty, "Congress Wasting Time on Steroids in Baseball?" Cafferty File, February 13, 2008, http://caffertyfile. blogs.cnn.com/2008/02/13/congress-wasting-time-on-steroids-in-baseball.

41 Tom Verducci, "No End of the Inglorious Ordeal: Clemens' Rep Takes a Big Hit, but Saga is far from Over," SI.com, Feb-ruary 13, 2008, http://sportsillustrated. cnn.com/2008/writers/tom_verducci/ 02/13/verducci.hearings/index.html.

42 *Federal Register* 72, no. 231 (December 3, 2007): 67994.

43 Christopher Wellman, "Do Celebrated Athletes Have Special Responsibilities to be Good Role Models? An Imagined Dialogue between Charles Barkley

and Karl Malone," in *Sports Ethics: An Anthology*, ed. Jan Boxhill, 333–336 (London: Blackwell, 2003).

44 Floyd Landis, *Positively False: The Real Story of How I Won the Tour de France* (New York: Simon Spotlight Entertain-ment, 2007), 200.

45 House Committee on Energy and Com-merce, Subcommittee on Commerce, Trade, and Consumer Protection, *Drugs in Sports: Compromising the Health of Athletes and Undermining the Integrity of Competition*, 110th Congress, 2nd Session, February 27, 2008, submitted testimony of Roger Goodell and Gene Upshaw, 12–13.

46 Landis, *Positively False*, 225.

47 House Committee, *Drugs in Sports*, sub-mitted testimony of David Stern, 11–12.

48 U.S. Const. amend IV.

49 *Skinner v. Railway Labor Executives' Association*, 489 U.S. 602, 624 (1989).

50 *Ibid.*

51 *Treasury Employees v. Von Raab*, 489 U.S. 656 (1989).

52 *Vernonia School Dist. 47J v. Acton*, 515 U.S. 646 (1995).

53 *Chandler v. Miller*, 520 U.S. 305 (1997).

54 Charles V. Dale, *Federally Mandated Drug Testing in Professional Athletics: Constitutional Issues* (Congressional Research Service Report RL32911, 2005), 6.

55 *Chandler v. Miller.*

56 *Chandler v. Miller, citing Olmstead v. United States*, 277 U.S. 438 (1928) (Brandeis, J., dissenting).

57 *Chandler v. Miller.*

58 House Committee, *Drugs in Sports*, sub-mitted testimony of Donald Fehr, 13–14.

Counterpoint: Congressional Intervention Is Needed to Restore Public Confidence in Professional Sports

59 House Committee, *Restoring Faith in America's Pastime*, 242.

60 *Ibid.*, 227.

61 *Ibid.*, 56.

62 Dale, *Federally Mandated Drug Testing*, 6.

63 *Ibid.*

64 House Committee, *Steroids in Sports*, 25.

65 *Ibid.*, 25–26.
66 National Institute on Drug Abuse, *High School and Youth Trends* (Bethesda, Md.: National Institutes of Health, 2007), 5.
67 Senate Committee, *Steroid Use in Professional Baseball*, 2.
68 House Committee, *Restoring Faith in America's Pastime*, 56.
69 *Ibid.*
70 House Committee, *Drugs in Sports*, quoted in Associated Press, "Congress Addresses Steroids Again," February 27, 2008.
71 *Ibid.*
72 Canseco, *Juiced,* 200.
73 *Ibid.*
74 House Committee, *Drugs in Sports*, submitted testimony of Travis Tygart, 4–5.
75 *Ibid.*, 5.
76 *Ibid.*
77 *Ibid.*
78 John McCloskey and Julian Bailes, *When Winning Costs too Much: Steroids, Supplements, and Scandals in Today's Sports* (Lanham, Md.: Taylor Trade Publishing, 2005), 43.
79 *Ibid.*, 44
80 *Vernonia School District 47J v. Acton.*
81 *Ibid.*
82 *Ibid.*
83 *Ibid.*
84 *Shoemaker v. Handel*, 795 F.2d 1136 (3d Cir., 1986).
85 *Ibid.*
86 *Ibid.*
87 *Chandler v. Miller.*
88 *Ibid.*
89 *Ibid.*

Point: Athletes Need More Freedom to Take Dietary Supplements
90 *U.S. Anti-Doping Agency v. Piasecki*, AAA No. 30 190 00358 07, North American Court of Arbitration for Sport Panel, September 24, 2007.
91 *Ibid.*
92 *Ibid.*
93 *Ibid.*
94 *Ibid.*
95 *Ibid.*
96 *Ibid.*
97 *Ibid.*
98 Dietary Supplement Health and Education Act, Public Law No. 103–417, 103d Congress, 2d Session (1994).
99 *Ibid.*
100 Natural Products Association, "Separating Supplement Facts from Fiction," http://www.naturalproductsassoc.org/site/PageServer?pagename=ic_supplement_facts#Dietary%20Supplement%20Safety.
101 *Ibid.*
102 *Ibid.*
103 Tim N. Ziegenfuss, Michael Rogers, Lonnie Lowery, et al., "Effect of Creatine Loading on Anaerobic Performance and Skeletal Muscle Volume in NCAA Division 1 Athletes," *Nutrition* 18 (May 2002): 397–402.
104 NCAA Research Staff, *NCAA Study of Substance Use Habits of College Student-Athletes* (Indianapolis, Ind.: National Collegiate Athletic Association, 2001).
105 NCAA Bylaw 16.5.2(g) (2007). See also "NCAA Issues Notice about Nutritional-Supplement Provision," *NCAA News Online*, May 23, 2005.
106 Layne Norton, "The Safety of Creatine," Bodybuilding.com, October 1, 2002, http://www.bodybuilding.com/fun/layne22.htm.
107 *Vencill v. U.S. Anti-Doping Agency*, Court of Arbitration for Sport, March 11, 2004.
108 Jessica K. Foschi, "A Constant Battle: The Evolving Challenges in the International Fight Against Doping in Sport," *Duke Journal of Comparative and International Law* 18 (2006): 457–486.
109 *Ibid.*
110 Natural Products Association Press Release, "Natural Products Association Issues Statement on MLB 'Mitchell Report,'" December 14, 2007.
111 House Committee on Government Reform, *The Regulation of Dietary Supplements: A Review of Consumer Safeguards*, 109th Congress, 2d Session, March 9, 2006, 16.
112 *Ibid.*, 17–18.
113 Natural Products Association Press Release.
114 House Committee, *The Regulation of Dietary Supplements*, 18.

◀▐▏▏▏▏ NOTES

Counterpoint: Dietary Supplements Are Harmful to Athletes and Athletic Competition

115 David Klossner, ed., *Sports Medicine Handbook 2006–2007* (Indianapolis, Ind.: National Collegiate Athletic Association, 2006), 41.

116 *Ibid.*

117 U.S. Anti-Doping Agency, "Supplements & Sanctions: A Cautionary Tale," *Spirit of Sport* 8, no. 1 (January–March 2008): 1–2.

118 *U.S. Anti-Doping Agency v. Piasecki.*

119 Michael S. Schmidt, "Cameron Suspended for Violating Stimulant Policy," *New York Times*, November 1, 2007, http://www.nytimes.com/2007/11/01/sports/baseball/01steroids.html.

120 Assael, *Steroid Nation*, 158.

121 Canseco, *Juiced*, 204.

122 *Vencill v. U.S. Anti-Doping Agency.*

123 McCloskey and Bailes, *When Winning Costs too Much*, 104.

124 Assael, *Steroid Nation*, 157.

125 House Committee, *The Regulation of Dietary Supplements*, 189.

126 *Ibid.*

127 U.S. Food and Drug Administration, letter to Ryan R. DeLuca, July 7, 2006.

128 See http://www.ergopharm.net/products_6oxo.php.

129 McCloskey and Bailes, *When Winning Costs too Much*, 104.

130 *Ibid.*, 105.

Conclusion: The Future of Doping

131 Associated Press, "WADA Chief says Reliable HGH Test will be Set up in Time for Summer Games," February 27, 2008.

132 World Anti-Doping Agency, "Q&A: Human Growth Hormone Testing," 2007, http://www.wada-ama.org/en/dynamic.ch2?pageCategory.id=627.

133 *USA Today*/Gallup Poll, "Baseball Fans: Clemens Lied about Steroid Use," February 29, 2008.

134 Tom Fitzgerald, "Should Bonds Be in the Hall of Fame," *San Francisco Chronicle*, March 10, 2006, http://www.sfgate.com/cgi-bin/article.cgi?f=/chronicle/archive/2006/03/10/SPGA3HM05L1.DTL.

135 *Ibid.*

136 Joan Walsh, "Your Cheating Stars," *Salon*, December 21, 2007, http://www.salon.com/opinion/walsh/2007/12/21/bonds/index.html.

Books and Reports

Assael, Shaun. *Steroid Nation: Juiced Home Run Totals, Anti-Aging Miracles, and a Hercules in Every High School: The Secret Story of America's True Drug Addiction.* New York: ESPN Books, 2007.

Canseco, Jose. *Juiced: Wild Times, Rampant 'Roids, Smash Hits, and How Baseball Got Big.* New York: Regan Books, 2005.

Dale, Charles V. *Federally Mandated Drug Testing in Professional Athletics: Constitutional Issues.* Congressional Research Service Report RL32911. 2005.

Fainaru-Wada, Mark, and Lance Williams. *Game of Shadows: Barry Bonds, BALCO, and the Steroids Scandal that Rocked Professional Sports.* New York: Gotham Books, 2006.

Landis, Floyd. *Positively False: The Real Story of How I Won the Tour de France.* New York: Simon Spotlight Entertainment, 2007.

McCloskey, John, and Julian Bailes. *When Winning Costs too Much: Steroids, Supplements, and Scandals in Today's Sports.* Lanham, Md.: Taylor Trade Publishing, 2005.

Mitchell, George J. *Report to the Commissioner of Baseball of an Independent Investigation into the Illegal Use of Steroids and Other Performance Enhancing Substances by Players in Major League Baseball.* December 13, 2007.

World Anti-Doping Agency. *Tour de France 2003: Independent Observer Report.* Montreal, Quebec: World Anti-Doping Association, 2003.

Web sites

Bodybuilding.com
http://www.bodybuilding.com
Web site catering to bodybuilders, generally supporting the use of muscle-building supplements (including some articles praising steroids) and offering opinions that conflict with many established medical and institutional viewpoints.

Computer Access to Research on Dietary Supplements (CARDS) Database
http://dietary-supplements.info.nih.gov/Research/CARDS_Database.aspx
Computer database on research about dietary supplements, maintained by the National Institutes of Health, a government agency.

Court of Arbitration for Sport

http://www.tas-cas.org
> International organization that mediates sports-related disputes, including appeals of doping test results and sanctions. Maintains a catalogue of previous decisions.

Drug Enforcement Agency

http://www.usdoj.gov/dea
> Federal agency responsible for enforcing the Anabolic Steroid Control Act and other drug laws. Links to federal drug laws and publications explaining the hazards of performance-enhancing drug use, particularly information geared toward teens and student-athletes.

Food and Drug Administration

http://www.fda.gov
> Federal agency responsible for enforcing laws related to dietary supplements. Includes regulatory information and information for the public about dietary supplement use.

National Center for Drug-free Sport

http://www.drugfreesport.com
> Provides education and drug-testing services to sports organization. Offers articles about testing and doping issues.

National Collegiate Athletic Association

http://www.ncaa.org
> Governing body for intercollegiate sports. Includes information about testing policy and articles of interest to student-athletes.

National Football League Players Association

http://www.nflpa.org
> Labor union representing NFL players. Site contains extensive information about the league's drug-testing program.

National Library of Medicine, dietary supplements page

http://sis.nlm.nih.gov/enviro/dietarysupplements.html
> Links to numerous sources of reliable information about the safety and effectiveness of dietary supplements.

Natural Products Association

http://www.naturalproductsassoc.org
> Industry group representing manufacturers of dietary supplements and other products. Promotes the legislative interests of supplement manufacturers and offers information about individual dietary supplements.

U.S. Anti-Doping Agency

http://www.usantidoping.org
> Organization devoted to conducting drug testing, making eligibility determinations, and educating American athletes about doping. Site contains information about prohibited substances and newsletters for athletes.

World Anti-Doping Agency

http://www.wada-ama.org

Governing and policy-making body for anti-doping agencies. Web site contains official list of prohibited substances and information about testing and eligibility decisions.

PICTURE CREDITS

PAGE

13: AP Images/Reed Saxon

17: AP Images/Santilli

33: AP Images

49: AP Images/Francois Duckett

62: AP Images/Mary Altaffer

73: AP Images/Julie Jacobson

118: AP Images/Ed Degasero

ALAN MARZILLI, M.A., J.D., lives in Birmingham, Alabama, and is a program associate with Advocates for Human Potential, Inc., a research and consulting firm based in Sudbury, Massachusetts, and Albany, New York. He primarily works on developing training and educational materials for agencies of the federal government on topics such as housing, mental health policy, employment, and transportation. He has spoken on mental health issues in 30 states, the District of Columbia, and Puerto Rico; his work has included training mental health administrators, nonprofit management and staff, and people with mental illnesses and their families on a wide variety of topics, including effective advocacy, community-based mental health services, and housing. Marzilli has written several handbooks and training curricula that are used nationally and as far away as the U.S. territory of Guam. Additionally, he managed statewide and national mental health advocacy programs and worked for several public interest lobbying organizations while studying law at Georgetown University. Marzilli has written more than a dozen books, including numerous titles in the *Point/Counterpoint* series.